# BREITLING
# 140 YEARS IN 140 STORIES

BREITLING
1884

# 140 YEARS IN 140 STORIES

RIZZOLI
NEW YORK

New York · Paris · London · Milan

# STORIES

18
84

## 1884 – 1914
## The founding era

19
14



19
14

## 1914 – 1932
## Revolutionary innovation

19
32



19
32

## 1932 – 1979
## The era of vision

19
79

19
79

# 1979 – 1994
## A new beginning

19
94



19
94

# 1994 – 2017
## State of the art

20
17



20
17

# 2017 – 2024
## A modern-retro brand

20
24

## ABOUT THIS BOOK

Welcome to *140 Years in 140 Stories*, a journey through Breitling's illustrious 140-year history. Beginning in Leon Breitling's modest Swiss workshop in 1884, this book charts the evolution of a brand synonymous with luxury watchmaking on a global scale. The collection is presented in 140 distinct stories, each one offering a singular snapshot from Breitling's history. Designed for both the casual enthusiast and the aficionado, it invites you to engage with the stories, however you choose, whether that's a linear progression or a random selection. What makes this book truly special is the unveiling of little-known and sometimes never-before-seen documents, photographs, and vintage watches. It's a first-time glimpse into hidden treasures from Breitling's past, making it not just a recounting of history, but a reveal of the brand's defining moments. The creation of *140 Stories* was a yearlong collaborative effort, encompassing insights from Breitling's historian, past and present employees, celebrity ambassadors, collectors, friends of the brand, and the Breitling family. Together, they have crafted a narrative that resonates with the brand's ethos of "casual, conscious luxury with purpose and a touch of fun." As you turn these pages, you will experience that spirit, and see not just how far the brand has come, but how far it plans to go. Ready to get started? Flip to the beginning—or jump in anywhere.

18
84

19
14

## 1884-1914
# THE FOUNDING ERA

Leon Breitling was destined to be a watchmaker. He grew up in La Chaux-de-Fonds, the center of the Swiss watchmaking universe, surrounded by the small family workshops that fabricated cases, dials, hands, springs, crowns, and screws for local *établisseurs* [assemblers] who made them into finished timepieces.
His uncle was a watchmaker, and Leon would spend time as a boy in the workshop, peering over the shoulders of the workers. As soon as he was old enough, he apprenticed with a chronograph specialist in nearby Renan, which marked the beginning of a lifelong passion. In 1884, at the age of 24, Leon set up his own chronograph workshop, first in Saint-Imier and then back in his hometown of La Chaux-de-Fonds, where he shared a factory with another chronograph maker.
Leon's legacy was considerable. In his quest to innovate and improve upon the complication that captivated him, he helped shape the chronograph as we know it today. In 1889, he filed a patent for a simplified movement with a single wheel and modified toothing that made it easier to manufacture. Toward the end of his life, he put in place the research and prototypes that would allow his son, Gaston, to engineer a chronograph with an independent pushpiece at two o'clock that could start, stop, and reset the chronograph. It was a milestone development, not just for Breitling but for the chronograph in general.

# I

## LEON BREITLING: BUILDING A LEGEND

Founder Leon Breitling wasn't the first member of his family to put the Breitling name on a watch. His grandparents were originally from Gechingen, a small village in Württemberg, near Stuttgart, but migrated to the Swiss Jura Mountains around the beginning of the nineteenth century. They first settled in Les Ponts-de-Martel, one of the earliest farmer-watchmaker villages, and later moved to La Chaux-de-Fonds. Leon's grandfather Jacob-Martin and his wife had 14 children. He was a *boulanger et cabaretier* [baker-taverner] by trade. Leon's father, also named Jacob, went on to work for the Swiss railway, which, as anyone who has ever traveled in Switzerland knows, always runs precisely on time. One of his uncles, Charles-Auguste, married into the Laederich family of watchmakers and in 1850 established the Breitling-Laederich company, specializing in high-end gold pocket watches, some with enamel dials and engraved cases. Many were exported to America, introducing the family to those channels of trade, and giving Leon his first exposure as a youngster to the workings of a watchmaker's workshop.

# 2

## BORN INTO TIMEKEEPING

How did an enclave of sleepy villages in the Swiss Jura Mountains become the cradle of watchmaking? It started with farmers. During the long winter months, when the fields were covered with snow and the livestock was hunkered down in the barn, there was less to do around the farm. The women turned to tatting lace to pass the time and earn some extra income, while the men made clocks and clock components in home workshops. What began in the mid-eighteenth century with basic clockmaking progressed to pocket watches and then complications. Some of the farmers would travel to Geneva to study watchmaking and then return to the valley to share their knowledge and skills. By the mid-1880s, a number of small workshops had sprung up in the Jura towns of La Chaux-de-Fonds and Saint-Imier, producing cases, crowns, hairsprings, escapements, hands, dials, screws, and other parts. Leon Breitling was born in 1860 in La Chaux-de-Fonds, the heart of this industrious community.

*ABOVE*
*Site of Leon Breitling's first watchmaking workshop at Place Neuve in Saint-Imier*

# 3

## START TIME: 1884

After completing an apprenticeship with a chronograph maker in the small town of Renan, near La Chaux-de-Fonds, Leon Breitling took his chances by opening his own workshop. He pushed the start button on "Leon Breitling, Fabricant" in 1884, setting up a shop in Saint-Imier, in the Bernese Jura. What only four years earlier had been a modest farm village with a population of 800, had mushroomed to 7,500 inhabitants by the time of Leon's arrival. Most of them worked in small, specialized workshops producing watch components largely by hand. Leon decided the chronograph represented the future, and started out of the gate making precision timers for competitive sports, an area of rapid growth—in fact, the first international Olympics was just over a decade away, in 1896. Leon foresaw a market for chronographs that applied to sport, industry, technical trades, the sciences, and any other activities that required state-of-the-art precision. His goal was to make useful, functional, reliable instruments rather than the decorative pieces many of his contemporaries were producing. Leon's Saint-Imier atelier was a one-man operation, but he soon arranged a return to his hometown of La Chaux-de-Fonds, where he would take up residence in a factory with another chronograph maker of the period, Couleri-Meri, giving him the means to scale up. And so the adventure began.

# 4

## KING OF THE COLUMN WHEEL

Since Leon Breitling was a maker of chronographs, it made sense that his first logo included a column wheel, the uber-device that controls the action in a high-quality chronograph mechanism, governing the start, stop, and reset-to-zero functions. At least, it would have made sense if it were at all common for companies in 1800 to have logos—or if the end user was likely to recognize the part. At the center of the motif, Leon added his own initials. It was a bold move, the proud signature of a newly minted creator of precision timekeeping instruments.

*BELOW*
*Leon Breitling's first logo (left) was based on the shape of the chronograph column wheel, shown (right) from the modern Breitling Manufacture Caliber 01*

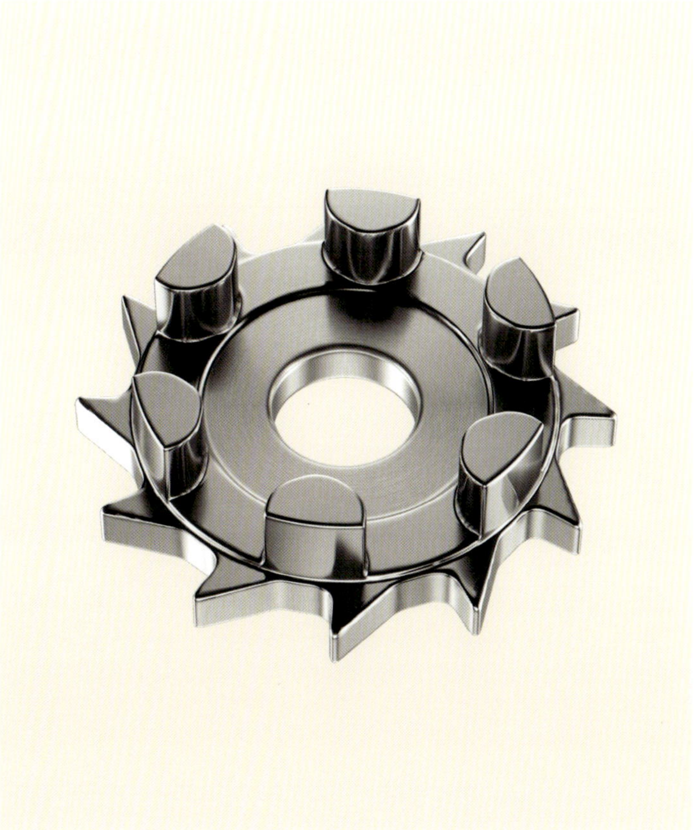

PLAN
DE
LA CHAUX DE FONDS
AVEC
LES ALIGNEMENTS ET NIVELLEMENTS FIXÉS
dressé au 1. Mars 1887
par la Direction des Travaux publics
et mis à jour au 1er Mars 1893.
BOULEVARD DU PETIT CHATEAU
BOULEVARD DE LA FONTAINE
TERRITOIRE DES EPLATURES
BOULEVARD DES CRÊTETS
Sur les Sentiers
Les Crêtets
Le Pré Jaquet Droz
Beau Site
Le Crêt des Olives
Le Couvent
Rue Leopold Robert
PLACE DE L'OUEST
Collège industriel
Collège primaire

LEFT
*An 1893 map of La Chaux-de-Fonds shows how the streets were arranged in neat, south-facing rows, so its workshops were exposed to maximum daylight*

# 5

## THE HEARTBEAT OF HOROLOGY: LA CHAUX-DE-FONDS

In 1892, Leon Breitling moved his headquarters back to his hometown of La Chaux-de-Fonds, which by then had become the center of Swiss watchmaking—a town planned with the same measure of precision that goes into crafting a watch movement. Its rows of streets were arranged in parallel lines, on a slight incline, and at set distances calculated to receive maximum daylight. Workshops were mostly on the brighter upper floors, with residences on the lower levels. In between the buildings were gardens, designed with pleasant views and a healthy work-life balance in mind. Karl Marx saw La Chaux-de-Fonds as a triumph of collective industry, referring to it in *Das Kapital* as "a single watch manufactory." Willy Breitling, Leon's grandson, would later comment, "Once a simple village with solid and rustic houses, it is now a large city bristling with factories and ateliers. It's a modern city: the metropolis of Swiss and world watchmaking."
La Chaux-de-Fonds, which also produced such industrious inhabitants as architect Charles-Edouard Jeanneret, better known as Le Corbusier, and automobile mogul Louis Joseph Chevrolet, was named a UNESCO World Heritage site in 2009.

1884

1914

# 6

# MONTBRILLANT: A HOME AND A FACTORY

Aside from the family name, few other words are more closely associated with the Breitling brand than Montbrillant. It was Breitling's first factory, named after the street where it was located: 3, Rue de Montbrillant. Founder Leon Breitling opened it in 1892 after returning to La Chaux-de-Fonds. It marked the beginning of Breitling's evolution from a small, cottage workshop to an industrial enterprise, in a building that would remain the beating heart of Breitling's production for decades to come. The factory, which Breitling shared with Couleri-Meri, another chronograph maker of the period, occupied the center of the structure, incorporating two stories of watchmaking workshops with huge picture windows that provided optimum light. But Montbrillant was also a place to live. At each end of the factory section were villas with large windows and French-style mansard roofs. The west wing was home to three generations of Breitlings, who lived alongside the bustling enterprise. The area was not industrial, as you would imagine a factory location today. It was adjacent to Parc Montbrillant, a serene greenspace that Leon loved so much he renamed the company "L. Breitling, Montbrillant Watch Manufactory."

The building had pride of place in Breitling's advertisements, and even appeared for a time on the company's letterhead. Brochures often showed images of the building, including a large smoke stack in a section that Breitling never actually occupied. The story goes that Leon liked to include it as a symbol of the emerging industrial revolution and the key role his company would play as a timekeeper to industry's progress. Montbrillant would do that and more—it would flourish for over 80 years as Breitling's manufacturing headquarters.

*TOP*
*Leon Breitling made the manufactory name his logo*

*ABOVE*
*Leon's children, Gaston and Angele*

*RIGHT*
*The Breitlings' living quarters were attached to the workshop*

# 7

## BUILT FOR SPEED

To Leon Breitling, the chronograph represented the future. The industrial revolution was in full swing, and it was the dawn of the scientific management theory of Taylorism, where every step of the industrial manufacturing process was timed to optimize output. Industry was moving faster, trains were moving faster, and so were people. Changing lifestyles meant more leisure time, and a burgeoning category of sportspeople who needed chronographs to time their new exploits, whether it was cycling, driving cars, riding motorcycles, or taking in the horseraces. Leon saw this new world of speed as an area of specialty he was going to capture.

# Taylorism

*Noun*

A scientific management theory that analyzes and synthesizes workflows by isolating and timing each process, allowing employees to complete assignments as efficiently as possible. It was devised by Frederick Winslow Taylor, an American mechanical engineer and management consultant. Taylorism required the use of a stopwatch, and that's where Breitling came in.

# 9

## EARLY BRANDING

Breitling was one of the first watch companies to brand its dials—not by name, at first, but by function. Leon Breitling began applying motifs to his watches, registering his first horseracing logo in 1896 (later called the Longchamps) and a cycling logo (the Salvator). He also registered logos for the speed-measuring Vitesse, along with Sprint and Montbrillant for subsequent models. Although the Breitling name was featured in advertisements around that time, it wasn't until the 1920s that the brand mark began to appear on dials and, even then, only on a few rare enamel pieces.

*ABOVE*
***The Longchamps horseracing pocket watch (left) and Salvator for cycling***

# 10

## SIMPLIFY AND EXPAND

When Leon Breitling grew his operation from a small workshop to the Breitling Manufactory in 1892, he was consciously going up against the emerging industrialization of American watchmaking. Their mass production system allowed them to produce huge numbers of watches at very competitive prices. Leon knew he had to compete, but instead of going full industrial, he aimed for the perfect balance of machine and manual production—quality as well as quantity. Still, his output was prodigious. By the early 1900s, Breitling was producing not only sophisticated chronographs, but complications like phonotelemeters, tachymeters, medical pulsometers, and rattrapantes.

Leon protected his advancements by being an early adopter of patents, filing with the newly established Swiss Federal Institute of Intellectual Property. To show just how quick-on-the-draw he was, Leon's first patent, filed in 1889, held the number 927. It was for a simplified chronograph timer with a single wheel and normal toothing. This was followed in 1891 by another patent, for an "observation chronograph-timer" with a triple control that could be activated using the crown. It "differs from existing systems in its simplicity, and its ease of manufacture, and especially repair outside the country," he proclaimed. It was another step toward the mass production of chronographs, the idea being to reduce costs by simplifying the mechanism, while protecting his advancements from potential imitators.

*L. Breitling, Montbrillant Watch Manufactory.* Brevet N° **34871.**
*1 feuille.*

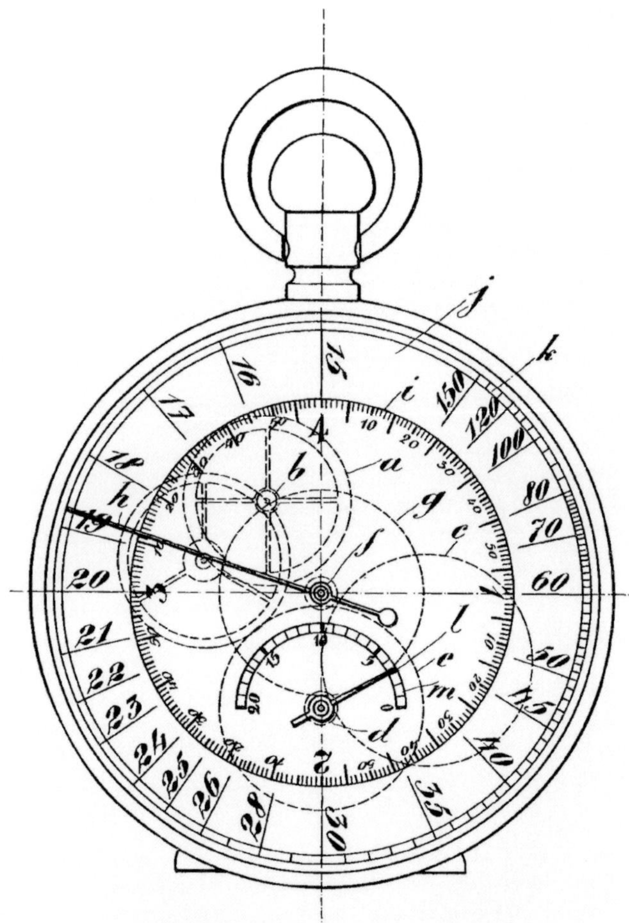

*ABOVE*
*To safeguard his innovations, Leon Breitling became an early adopter of patents*

# II

## PIONEERING PROMOTIONS

"Our chronographs are always the most appreciated, because their mechanisms are simple and rugged, their functions irreproachable, their shapes elegant, their prices among the lowest." So proclaimed an early 1900s Breitling advertisement, one of the first in a series of ads to raise the company's profile among its target audience: people who used watches as timing tools. In a display of early marketing strategy, Leon's innovations gained fame by his use of a form of publicity known as *réclame*, or "claims." In the first issue of the *Revue Internationale de l'Horlogerie et des Branches Annexes,* published in January 1900, a Breitling ad sang the praises of its sports timers and chronographs. This included its model with a split-seconds hand for timing events with different end times, as well as a newly launched "8-day power reserve," a table clock that could run for over a week without being wound. In another ad from 1906, the company proudly boasted: "More than 100,000 chronographs and timers in use in all countries." In 1911, Leon called attention to his prolific production of split-seconds instruments— "growing daily, which is the proof of their unmatched superiority." Fortunately, Leon had the innovative products to back up his "claims."

*ABOVE*
*"More than 100,000 chronographs and timers in use in all countries" heralds a Breitling ad from 1906*

1884

# 12

1914

1907

# VITESSE

## EARLY POLICE RADAR

In the late nineteenth century, everything started moving faster: cars, trains, athletes, and industry. The Vitesse [French for "speed"] was all about timing the new pace of life. It was a complex chronograph with a tachymeter scale that could measure and display speeds from 15 to 250 kilometers per hour. It became a favorite instrument of Swiss police to catch speeding drivers [yes, you have Breitling to thank for that innovation]—early evidence of Breitling's indispensability as a tool watch.

19
14

19
32

## 1914-1932
# REVOLUTIONARY INNOVATION

Leon Breitling's son, Gaston, led the company for only 13 years, but in that short time made a lasting impact. Less than a year after he took over from his father in 1914, Gaston launched a chronograph that completely changed the game and would define how wrist chronographs still function today. It had an independent pushpiece at two o'clock to start, stop, and reset the chronograph. It was revolutionary, considering that wrist chronographs at the time were really just pocket watches attached to wristlets or with soldered wire lugs, with all functions controlled by a crown at 12 o'clock. His next step was to file a patent in 1923 for a chronograph that offered an independent start and pause pusher and an additional independent reset activator in one of the crown positions. It was the first patented chronograph with start, stop, pause, restart, and stop activated by a separate reset-to-zero actuator, truly a breakthrough development. Gaston Breitling's time at the helm of his family business was short, but his legacy was large.

# 13

## CHANGING HANDS: LEON BREITLING TO GASTON BREITLING

Leon Breitling died in August 1914 at the age of 54—it's hard to believe how much he accomplished in such a short lifetime. His son, Gaston, already groomed to take over the business, quietly renamed the company "G.-Leon Breitling Montbrillant Watch Manufactory," a subtle way of noting the succession while paying homage to his father through the emphasis on his middle name. Leon left behind a prosperous business, but his death came just a few days after the start of World War I, which plunged Europe into economic turmoil. Markets closed, raw materials were in short supply, transport and payment difficulties abounded. Gaston navigated these turbulent times with aplomb, starting with the introduction of Breitling's first great contribution to the development of the modern chronograph: the independent pushpiece.

LA DOMENICA DEL CORRIERE

| | NEL REGNO | ESTERO |
|---|---|---|
| Anno | L. 5 — | L. 10 — |
| Semestre | » 2,50 | » 5 — |

Si pubblica a Milano ogni Domenica
Supplemento illustrato del "Corriere della Sera"

Uffici del giornale:
Via Solferino, N. 28
MILANO

Per tutti gli articoli e illustrazioni è riservata la proprietà letteraria e artistica, secondo le leggi e i trattati internazionali.

Anno XVI. — Num. 27. 5 - 12 Luglio 1914. Centesimi 10 il numero.

L'assassinio a Serajevo dell'arciduca Francesco Ferdinando erede del trono d'Austria, e di sua moglie.
(Disegno di A. Beltrame).

*ABOVE*
*Cover of the Italian newspaper* La Domenica del Corriere *depicting the attack on Archduke of Austria Franz Ferdinand's motorcade, precipitating the start of World War I*

# 14

## WORLD WAR WATCHES

In 1914 World War I broke out after the assassination of Austrian Archduke Franz Ferdinand by a Serbian radical, setting off a chain of events that sent the world into turmoil. Austria-Hungary declared war on Serbia. Russia sided with the latter. Germany declared war on Russia, then attacked France, pulling Britain and eventually Japan, Italy, and the U.S. into the fray. By the time the carnage ended, it had claimed the lives of 17 million people and wreaked havoc on the European and world economies. In the midst of World War I's economic ruin, Breitling carved a niche by supplying soldiers with wrist-worn chronographs, which were crucial for timing battle plans. This focus on military utility allowed the company to secure a foothold in a market where many others stumbled into insolvency.

19
14

19
32

# 15

1915

# THE SINGLE PUSHER

## A FRESH START

Less than a year after Gaston Breitling took over his father's company, he dropped a bombshell of a watch that would forever change the way chronographs were designed. It was the first wrist-worn timepiece with a pusher at two o'clock that could start, stop, and reset the chronograph seconds, independent of the winding crown.
For Breitling, it was also a well-timed success story that helped carry the company through the uncertain war years and beyond.

ABOVE
*Wearable timepieces had found favor with women long before they appeared on men's wrists*

# 16

## FROM ORNAMENTAL TO INDISPENSABLE

In 1915, a wristwatch for men was still considered an oddity. That year, delegates to the 10th annual convention of the National Retail Jewelers Association in New York City debated whether wristwatches for men could even be deemed proper. One member remarked, "There's some excuse for a woman wearing her watch on her wrist... but a man has no such excuse. He has plenty of pockets." Another asserted, "The wrist watch will never be a common timepiece." Alas, World War I was escalating, and their predictions were to fall short. Armies had to coordinate precision attacks, and officers and soldiers alike needed to synchronize their watches.

On the battlefield, every second counted. Fumbling in one's waistcoat for a pocket watch could mean the difference between life and death. And so the wristwatch became an indispensable tool in wartime, but Gaston Breitling's advancement took it further. While most chronographs at the time were activated by pressing the crown at 12 o'clock, his wrist-worn chronograph with an independent pushpiece was a revolutionary development. It had a secure strap, with a winding crown at three o'clock and a chronograph pusher at two. That made it a convenient, potentially lifesaving tool to wear and use, in and out of the trenches.

# 17

## THE PUSHPIECE PERFECTED

Gaston Breitling went on to improve upon his independent chronograph-pusher design in 1923. It was a major innovation, which he was careful to patent. Based on his invention of 1915, it retained the principle of the separate pushpiece at two o'clock, but this pusher now controlled only the start-stop function, while the instrument was reset to zero by pulling on the crown. In addition, a safety system prevented the chronograph from being reset while its hands were in motion. This technical improvement, though invisible at first sight, created new possibilities to all kinds of users regardless of their field of endeavor, and provided the functionality later optimized in 1934 with Breitling's introduction of the dual pusher. It was now possible to time several events in succession, whether for a sports competition or an industrial process, without necessarily having to reset the instrument.

CONFÉDÉRATION SUISSE

BUREAU FÉDÉRAL DE LA PROPRIÉTÉ INTELLECTUELLE

**EXPOSÉ D'INVENTION**

Publié le 1er juillet 1924

**N° 105532** (Demande déposée: 14 septembre 1923, 17 h.) **Classe 71 k**

**BREVET PRINCIPAL**

G.-Léon BREITLING, MONTBRILLANT WATCH MANUFACTORY,
La Chaux-de-Fonds (Suisse).

**Chronographe.**

La présente invention se rapporte à un chronographe du genre de ceux comportant une roue à colonnes commandée par un poussoir indépendant de la couronne et produisant la mise en marche et l'arrêt de l'aiguille à secondes indépendante. Ce chronographe est caractérisé en ce que la remise à zéro de l'aiguille à secondes indépendante s'effectue par une traction sur la couronne de remontoir, traction qui ne peut s'opérer que lorsque l'aiguille est arrêtée. De cette façon, un actionnement accidentel de la couronne, pendant une observation, ne pourra pas se produire.

Le dessin ci-annexé représente, à titre d'exemple, une forme d'exécution de l'objet de l'invention.

*a* est la roue de champ du mouvement, tandis que *b* est la roue sur laquelle est montée l'aiguille de secondes indépendante. *c* est la roue du totalisateur de minutes et *d* est une roue à colonnes. *e* est une roue intermédiaire portée par le levier *f*; celui-ci est pivoté en $f^1$ et présente un talon $f^2$ coopérant avec les colonnes de la roue *d*. Un ressort $f^3$ tend constamment à maintenir ce levier dans la position représentée au dessin, position dans laquelle la roue *e* engrène avec la roue de champ *a* mais n'est pas en contact avec la roue *b*. A chaque tour de cette dernière roue, une saillie $b^1$, qu'elle porte, fait avancer d'une dent la roue $c^1$ qui, à son tour, fait avancer d'une dent la roue *c* du totalisateur. Celle-ci avance donc d'une dent à chaque tour de la roue du chronographe. La roue à colonnes *d* avance d'une dent chaque fois que l'on appuie sur le poussoir $d^1$, lequel actionne alors le cliquet $d^2$ d'avancement de la roue *d*. *h* est un marteau pivoté en $h^1$ et que le ressort $h^2$ tend constamment à maintenir dans la position représentée en traits pleins au dessin, position dans laquelle ses deux talons $h^3$ et $h^4$ sont éloignés des cœurs de remise à zéro fixés sur la roue du chronographe *b* et sur celle du totalisateur *c*. En tirant vers le haut la couronne de remontoir, on agit sur le levier $h^5$ lequel, à son tour, agit sur le marteau *h* et l'amène dans la position représentée en pointillé au dessin, position dans laquelle il agit sur les deux cœurs sus-mentionnés.

*LEFT*
*Gaston Breitling's patent for the 1923 improvement to his monopusher chronograph*

# 18

## WE DID THAT

# SINGING BIRDS

Gaston Breitling was a diligent marketer who chased every avenue of potential business for the brand, even if it meant veering off the chronograph path. For a time in the early 1900s, the company made *boîtes à oiseaux chanteurs*—singing bird boxes. These small, pin-and-cylinder music mechanisms were topped with automatons of specific birds who would tweet out tunes that accurately mimicked their calls. At the clients' request, Breitling could make examples that recreated the song of a nightingale, a warbler, or a goldfinch. The tiny birds resembled the real thing, especially when they opened their beaks to sing. According to family archives, these exotic chirpers were made in Paris by a Mr. Flajoulot, the brother of Gaston Breitling's wife, Berthe.

1932

1979

## 1932–1979
# THE ERA OF VISION

Willy Breitling took over the company in 1932 at the age of 19 and remained at the helm until his passing in 1979. He had a huge impact on Breitling, ushering it seamlessly into the modern era with finesse, introducing one innovation after another, and bringing his big personality to bear on everything he did. With respect for traditional watchmaking but with an eye to the future, Willy was responsible for most of the Breitling icons we know today: the elegant Premier, the iconic Navitimer, the seagoing SuperOcean, and the sporty Top Time. He found a way to fulfill his dream of taking chronographs to the masses, created a special division to develop cockpit instrumentation and pilot's watches during World War II, and added a touch of glamor to the chronograph in the postwar years. He pioneered the branding and marketing of watch collections, and he was one of the first to use sponsorships to connect his company to popular sporting events. Along the way, he had a lot of fun. Willy Breitling was a man who loved life. He could be seen driving ahead of competitors in the Breitling-sponsored Giro d'Italia race, testing his watches for water resistance in the waters near his home on Lake Geneva, or traveling Europe in his Bentley to share his passion for chronographs.

# 19

## CHANGING HANDS: GASTON BREITLING TO WILLY BREITLING

In 1927, Gaston Breitling died suddenly at the very young age of 43. His only son, Willy, was just 14 years old, and still in school. According to Swiss law, he had to wait until he turned 20 to be officially entered as the company administrator, and that was still six years away. For the next few years, Breitling was managed by his mother, Berthe, along with a succession of administrators who, as Willy later told his son, Gregory, "didn't always work in the company's best interest." Willy took charge officially in 1933 and, over the next 40 years, introduced one innovation after another and one iconic model after another. In the process, he clarified Breitling's specialty as a chronograph innovator. One of the first things he did was to revisit the 1923 patent his father had filed for the independent activation "start, pause, restart, stop, reset" function, and put it into production on every wrist chronograph. Willy would also become an ahead-of-his-time marketer, fully aware of the importance of the Breitling brand image, and as interested in "making it known" as he was in "knowing how to make it."

G.-Léon Breitling S. A.
Montbrillant Watch My

Brevet additionnel N° 175564
1 feuille

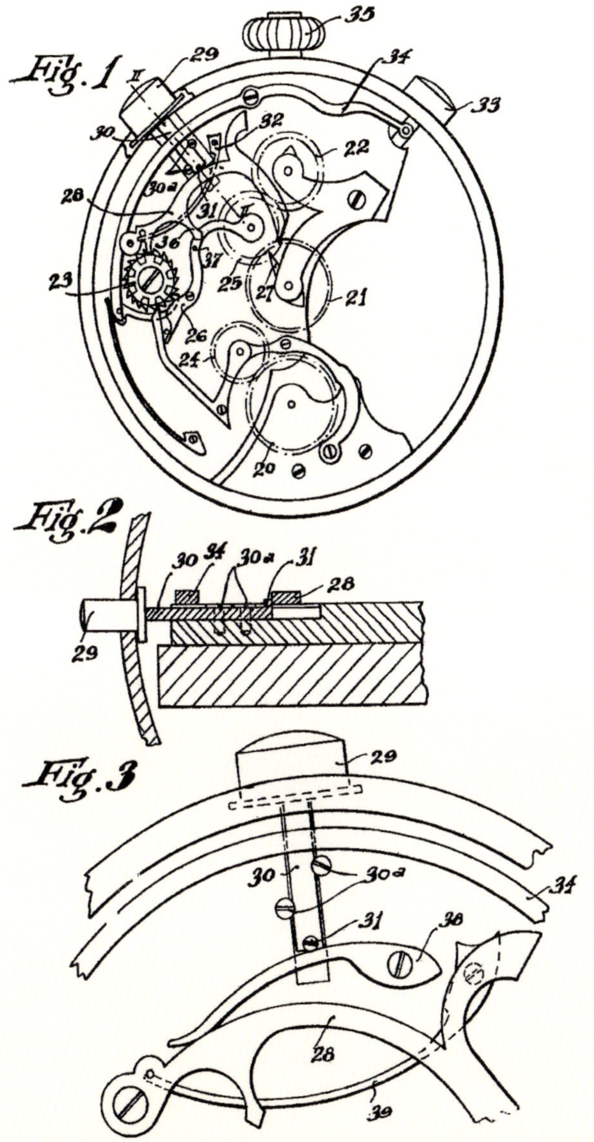


# 20

## EXCAVATING THE ARCHIVES

Willy Breitling's first order of business when he entered the company in 1932 was to comb the archives to gain a full understanding of what he had inherited and to find inspiration on how to move forward. It not only gave him a sense of the remarkable accomplishments of his father and grandfather, it motivated him to revisit one of them in particular. He revived the patent his father Gaston had filed in 1923 for the independent activation of the "start, pause, restart, stop, reset" actions, and decided it should be included on every Breitling wrist chronograph going forward. At the time, putting independent pushers at two and four that controlled all chronograph functions was revolutionary. Combining them with a movement small enough to fit the wrist was outstanding. Willy made it happen because he foresaw a quickly developing world where speed, sports, and changing lifestyles would make the wrist chronograph an indispensable tool for the masses—and he saw Breitling as the brand to do it.

*LEFT*
***Diagram to accompany the patent for the dual-pusher chronograph***

1932

# 21

1979

# 1934
# THE DUAL PUSHER
## TWO-FOUR TIMING

Willy Breitling combined his grandfather's stopwatch precision and his father's independent pusher innovation into a groundbreaking dual-pusher timepiece. If its shape looks familiar—one pushpiece at two o'clock to start, pause, restart, and stop the chrono; another at four to reset it—that's because it's still the way most chronographs work today. Think of it as a collaboration spanning three generations.

*LEFT*
*Kodak's affordable Brownie camera was the inspiration for Breitling's Populaires line*

# 22

## A KODAK MOMENT

An early Kodak product called the Brownie camera became the unlikely muse for Willy Breitling's corporate strategy. According to an interview Willy gave to an Austrian watch magazine in 1935, his vision for a "popular" chronograph was inspired by the example of the Brownie, which had revolutionized photography by transforming it from a professional pursuit into an everyday hobby for people. Kodak did it by producing simplified cameras with reduced functionality, thereby eliminating the barrier of unaffordable pricing. "We have to do something similar with chronographs," Willy told the publication. "We have to produce an entry-level product, affordable to everyone, that will make people aware that this was something they never thought they needed, but now know they do."

The simple, 60-second chronograph he was inspired to create shortly after giving that interview was the forerunner to an entry-level collection he called the Populaires. It proved very popular indeed, and Willy even branded the dial with the company logo—something most watch brands wouldn't start doing until much later—but which was precisely what Kodak had done with the Brownie.

ABOVE
*The Premier ref. 741, ca. 1936, featuring the Venus caliber 150*

# 23

## THE BIRTH OF VENUS

Not long after he took the reins of his family's company, Willy Breitling made the bold decision to change movement makers. Between 1935 and 1941, he phased out the ebauches made by the well-established Charles Hahn & Cie (later called Landeron-Hahn and then simply Landeron). In their place, he introduced calibers made by Venus, an up-and-coming manufacturer open to new ideas and modes of development, whom he came to see as a commercial kindred spirit. In Venus, Willy felt he had found a true partner in innovation, one that would help him fulfill his dreams of creating integrated chronograph complications. The Venus caliber families 15x and 17x column-wheel chronographs would be the base movement that powered most of Breitling's iconic watches in the decades to come, including the ref. 741, the root of the Premier line.

The Venus 170, with subdials at six and 12 o'clock, known as the "up-down" design, was the backbone of Breitling's mass-market Populaires range. Many people still describe the caliber 170 as the "Breitling movement," even when it was later used by other brands. Its successor was the caliber 188, later renamed the 7730 after Valjoux acquired Venus in 1966. That movement would evolve into Valjoux's famous 7750, one of the most recognizable and widely used automatic chronograph calibers in the business.

# 24

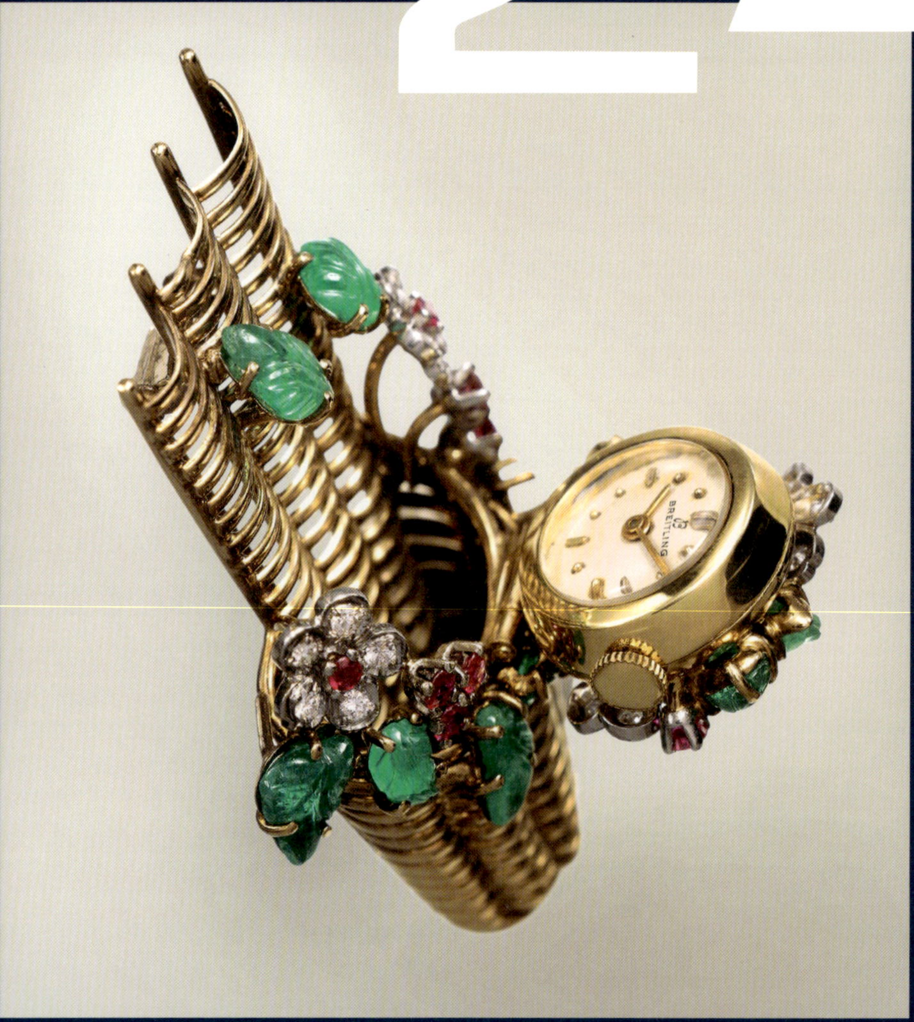

## WE DID THAT

# WOMEN'S COCKTAIL WATCHES

Throughout the 1940s and '50s Breitling rolled out an almost innumerable array of cocktail and jewelry watches, each design daintier and more elaborate than the next. But not all of these beauties were destined for the wrist: Breitling gave brooches, pendants, and even money clips an horological upgrade. Case in point, the Vigneronne, an evening-dress brooch crafted in 18 k gold, diamonds, rubies, and emeralds, described in its catalog entry as "a faithful reproduction of a Swiss grape-gatherer's pannier." Surely Willy Breitling had been inspired by the vineyards lining the steep banks of Lake Geneva when he created the striking ornament, whose floral bouquet turns on a hinge to reveal its concealed timepiece.

# 25

## NAME THAT WATCH

With a master plan of bringing the chronograph to the masses, Willy Breitling did something few watchmakers would have tried at the time: he branded his dials. Back then, it was mostly retailers who put their mark on watch dials since their names were known to end customers. Watch suppliers were expected to play an uncredited supporting role, providing so-called "sterile" dials that their merchants would then adapt. Willy took tentative steps toward changing that convention, adding model names, like Sprint (for its chronograph function) or Montbrillant (after the home of the Breitling manufactory). By the mid-1940s, he had clearly gotten the hang of it, and was unabashedly adding both the model name and a scripted Breitling logo for maximum brand recognition.

# 26

## STYLE STATEMENT OR SMOKESCREEN?

Willy Breitling leaned into his firm's commitment to creating tool-watch chronographs, but the market for them had yet to take hold beyond professional use. One of his efforts to tap into new market segments resulted in a puzzling late-1930s foray into decorative cases. Called Dernier Cri, the collection included elaborate and sometimes outlandish designs that overshadowed the chronograph function. The concept was undeniably off-base for Breitling, and yet Willy took the uncommon step of registering their designs to ward off potential imitators. Breitling historian Fred Mandelbaum holds the (as yet unproven) theory that Willy created and protected the designs in a smoke-and-mirrors move meant to distract competitors from the top-secret market he was actually pursuing: the burgeoning aircraft industry. Mandelbaum's rationale: "For all the pains Willy took to safeguard his unusual Dernier Cri designs, you cannot find a single, surviving example of most models."

*ABOVE*
***Willy Breitling may have been trying to distract competitors when he created the Dernier Cri***

19
32

19
79

# 27

## HUIT AVIATION

Breitling's status as an official supplier of cockpit instrumentation and pilot's watches was formalized in 1937, when the British War Office invited Willy Breitling to submit a production plan for the British Royal Air Force. For Willy, the invitation was a eureka moment that clarified his vision for the future of the Breitling brand. It became the impetus for his launch of the HUIT Aviation department in 1938, consolidating Breitling's status as an expert supplier of precision aircraft instrumentation. French for "eight," HUIT highlighted the exceptional eight-day power reserve its onboard clocks had at the time. Throughout World War II, demand soared for Breitling's flight instruments. They were tough timepieces, built to resist shocks, vibrations, magnetic forces, and temperature fluctuations. They were also highly readable, thanks to oversized numbers and hands, which were covered with luminescent paint that stood out against what were generally black dials to eliminate glare. In addition to the British RAF, the brand supplied other allied forces. Today, Breitling's most iconic collections, including the Navitimer and the Premier, honor the spirit—and the robustness—of these authentic aviation tools.

*BELOW*
*Publicity for the HUIT Aviation department*

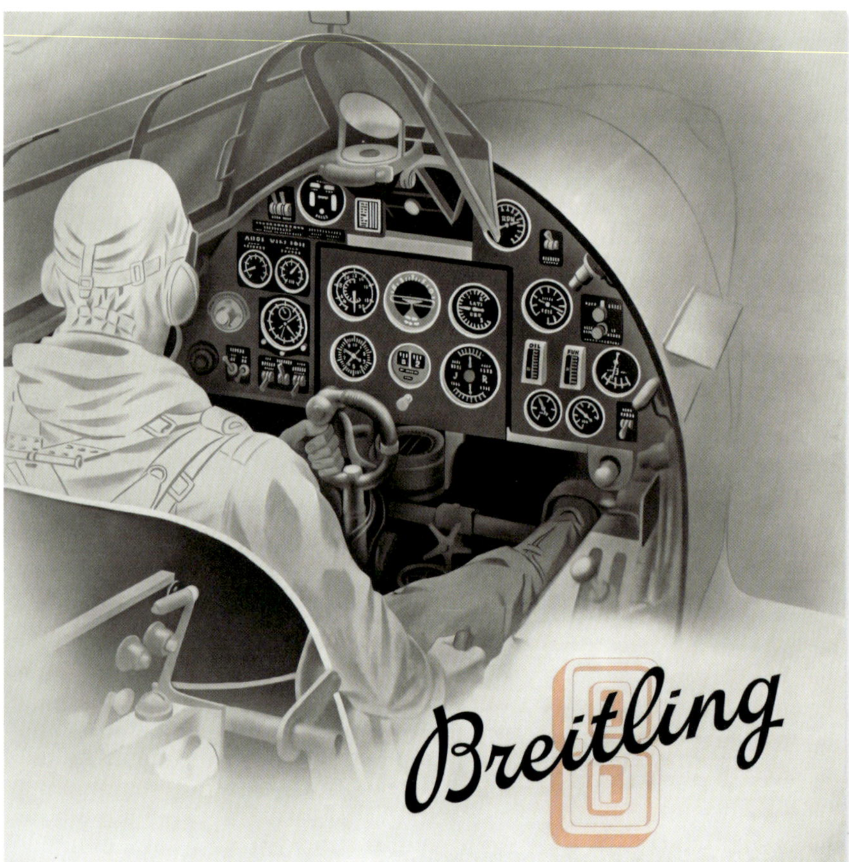


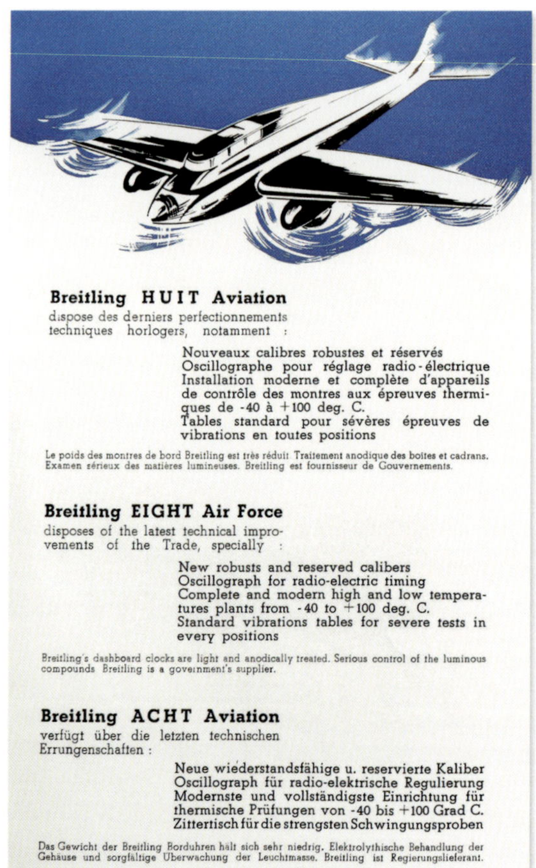

# 28

## COVERT OPS

Willy Breitling's cockpit-instrument deliveries to the Allies during World War II were spy-movie-worthy. He and his friends would take several cars at night to pastures in nearby Franches-Montagnes, in the Swiss Jura Mountains, where the cars would turn on their headlights to guide the Allied planes to landing. The pilots would quickly load the instruments and take off again. The operation, codenamed "Export under the fir trees," would end with Willy going into a busy pub in Geneva and getting drunk enough for people to remember seeing him that night. It seems Willy was a frequent visitor to the police station for disorderly conduct—all in the interest of his alibi. He's also said to have spirited equipment abroad using a diplomatic passport. And while we can't confirm all the rumors (Willy guarded his actions even from his own family), we do know that he was once tried unsuccessfully for smuggling.

1932

# 29

1979

# 1943
# HUIT PREMIER REF. 765
## THE FIRST PREMIER

Breitling's tool watch par excellence. These timepieces were built for wartime military precision and put to the test on specialized vibration tables that mimicked the punishing conditions of a warplane. The 38-millimeter waterproof case dwarfed the typical watch of the time. But once soldiers got used to its easy readability, they found it hard to downsize, making the Premier a hit in the postwar years as well.

Breitling
779
778
780

*LEFT*
*Film star Cesar Romero in a mid-1940s Breitling ad meant to set the stage for an era of postwar elegance*

19
32

19
79

# 30

## STAR POWER

In an era when celebrity endorsements were few and far between, forward-thinking Willy Breitling began stacking his campaigns with the stars. Cesar Romero, the suave 1940s film actor, was among the notables who appeared in advertisements for Breitling, under the caption "Years of Elegance." It marked the beginning of Willy's ambition to rebrand the chronograph from military tool watch to elegant gentleman's accessory, and conveyed a postwar optimism you could only find in the "pictures."

*RIGHT*
*Gifted watchmaker Marcel Robert was responsible for many Breitling advancements, including the wrist-worn slide rule*

# 31

## THE MAN BEHIND THE SCENES: MARCEL ROBERT

Willy Breitling worked hard to build his company's reputation and fortunes, but he didn't do it alone. He had the help of Marcel Robert, who joined the company in 1928 as a young watchmaker and became a trusted advisor to Gaston. When Willy took over the company in 1932, at the tender age of 19, he immediately appointed Robert as the company's technical director. When the company's administrative and sales offices were moved to Geneva in 1953, Robert stayed in La Chaux-de-Fonds, charged with running the Montbrillant manufactory.

In his nearly 50-year career with Breitling, Marcel Robert was instrumental in the company's success, playing a pivotal role in the development of its most important innovations, from the first patented dual-pusher caliber of 1933—whose early prototype he fashioned out of wood—to the slide rule on the Chronomat and Navitimer, to the co-development of the world's first automatic chronograph movement in 1969. When Robert celebrated his twenty-fifth anniversary with the company, Willy wrote this note to him: "I never felt alone in the struggle, and your presence at my side has always given me comfort and a sense of security."

19
32

19
79

# 32

1942

# CHRONOMAT 786

## A CHRONOGRAPH FOR MATHEMATICIANS

Breitling's first watch with a slide rule predated its more famous cousin, the Navitimer. When launched, the name stood for "chronograph for mathematicians" (not to be confused with modern versions, whose name is a combination of "chronograph" and "automatic"). One of Breitling's most beloved and enduring innovations, the slide rule is an analog calculator for the wrist.

# 33

## WILLY'S BABY: THE CHRONOMAT

Advertisements from 1942 and 1944 expressed the importance of Breitling's most enduring invention—the slide rule—as featured on the original Chronomat. So crucial was its launch to the company that one ad showed it in a crib, a reference to both the New Year and as an inside joke implying it was Willy Breitling's "baby." Other ads would take a more serious focus on the innovation, showing the array of mathematical calculations that were now at your wrist.

# 34 BEATRICE BREITLING'S TIMELESS INFLUENCE

*LEFT*
*A Breitling ad from 1953 may have been inspired by Willy Breitling's charismatic wife, Beatrice*

"My mother Beatrice was the unsung hero of Breitling. She was always there behind the scenes, which is ironic because, in life, she was a star of the stage. As one half of the dance duo Daisy & Ramon, she performed at the famous Parisian cabaret Le Drap d'Or that launched the careers of Edith Piaf, Gilbert Becaud, and many others.

Willy first laid eyes on her while she was on tour at the Moulin Rouge in Geneva. That night, she was extraordinary, and everyone—my father included—was captivated. Her onstage introduction had revealed that Beatrice was Hungarian. So Willy, determined to upstage the admirers who flocked to her after the show, seated himself at the piano and began to hammer out a famous Hungarian song. Beatrice was not impressed. She went to Willy and said, 'Monsieur, you're playing that song all wrong.' To which my father replied, 'I know. But it got you to talk to me, didn't it?' That's how they met and fell in love.

Beatrice became Willy's sounding board. He would always consult her when there was a new model in production. The best example is in the sixties when my father decided that he needed to attract young people to bring the chronograph back into fashion. He told us that the name of this youth-oriented watch would be Time Top. My mother smiled, said it was okay, 'But could I make a suggestion? I think you should change it around. Top Time would be catchier.' And that's precisely what he did. The watch went on to be a huge success, its memorable name being a part of its popularity. That was my mother: always sharp, always of the times. The epitome of grace and glamour."

**GREGORY BREITLING**

*The eldest son of Willy Breitling was immersed in the world of watchmaking from a young age. Today he represents the founding family, sharing his stories at Breitling events.*

# 35

PRECISION
Breitling
TELEMETRE
Breitling
PREMIER
SWISS MADE

## WE DID THAT
# SQUARE CHRONOS

Breitling's decision to add smaller cases and even square watches to its catalog in the 1940s may have been based on aesthetics, but it did nothing to compromise the brand's core purpose of functionality. The ref. 754, made around 1944, was equipped with a telemeter function in the first circular index, and a tachymeter scale on the innermost circular index. Analog hours were printed between the two circular scales, and a railroad chapter ring on the outer dial traced the square case shape. Naturally, it was also a chronograph, with minute totalizer and small seconds, driven by the Valjoux caliber R69, a small movement that was also used in round Premier models. All this in a petite steel case that measured a mere 27.6 by 26 millimeters.

*LEFT*
*The Premier ref. 754, ca. 1944, was a square-cased chrono, only 26 mm wide*

19
32

# 36

19
79

1945

# PREMIER 777

## STYLISH, ELEGANT, RELIABLE

If a single chronograph can ever sum up a legendary watchmaker, then the Triple Seven is surely Willy Breitling in all his brilliance. It carries off that most difficult of tricks: creating style out of function. Reliability honed for military accuracy is polished into a jewel to wear with swimming trunks, driving gloves, or a suit. To turn hardcore function into elegance, wartime necessity into longed-for luxury, is the achievement of genius.

19
32

19
79

# 37

## PREMIER
## DESIGN EVOLUTION

1943
### 734 HUIT
The first pilot's wristwatch from Breitling sets a lasting benchmark for the industry. A product of the HUIT Aviation department that will soon equip Royal Air Force war planes, it's the foundation of a new generation of chronographs.

1943
### DUOGRAPH 762
A huge technological breakthrough as Willy Breitling's determination to produce a rattrapante wristwatch pays off. Its complexity records multiple time intervals in style, but only 350 will be made over the next three decades.

1944
### DATORA 785
Willy Breitling predicts a postwar boom, and a resulting demand for ever-more complicated watches. His quest for new advances leads to a chronograph with day, month, and pointer date, available in steel or solid gold.

1967
### 765 AOPA
Sibling to Willy Breitling's beloved rattrapante, the waterproof ref. 765 has been a cornerstone of his catalog since the 1940s. Following the Navitimer's success as AOPA's official watch, the final 765s are presented to the association.

1998
### NAVITIMER PREMIER

Fast forward three decades. With Theodore Schneider at Breitling's helm, the Premier is relaunched while drawing on the prestige of the Navitimer name. Just 36 mm across, and with a revised subdial layout, it's a short-lived wonder.

2021
### PREMIER DATORA

A return to 1940s elegance as Georges Kern revives the moonphase with a full day-date chronograph. At 42 mm, it houses the manufacture caliber B25 developed with Concepto, channeling Willy Breitling's love of refined complications.

2021
### PREMIER DUOGRAPH

In steel or red gold, the stylish rattrapante is back, housing the complexity of Breitling's exclusive manufacture caliber B15. Hand wound, the Duograph has the square pushers and beautifully balanced split-seconds hand of the 1940s original.

2023
### PREMIER CHRONOGRAPH

Breitling gives its modern-retro treatment to the watch of "impeccable taste." Now it's equipped with the Breitling Manufacture Caliber 01 and features include the smooth fixed bezel and applied Arabic numerals of its tool-watch past.

19
32

19
79

# 38

## PREMIER B19 DATORA 42
## 140TH ANNIVERSARY

A celebration of the golden age, when purpose was transformed into style, drawing inspiration from 140 years of watchmaking. Based on the chronographs created for 1940s Allied air crews, it was a supreme expression of Willy Breitling's transformation of his rugged aviator's instrument into an elegant dress watch for everyday wear. The new in-house perpetual calendar B19 displays the day, month, date, and moonphase, housed in a solid red gold case, and limited to 140 pieces.

BREITLING
1884
TACHYMETER
SWISS MADE

# 39 WILLY BREITLING: AHEAD OF HIS TIME

"I had been a chronograph collector for many years without even knowing it. They were my personal everyday work tools for timing events. But being an inquisitive person, I started to dive into the history of the chronograph. My research made it clearer that Breitling was the defining factor in the evolution of this spectacular complication. The more I learned about the brand and the man behind it, Willy Breitling, the more I admired him. Everything was driven by his long-term vision. The guy was 19 years old when he took over the company and, from the start, he could see decades ahead. He saw the chronograph as a tool that everyone needed—one that was affordable, elegant, desirable. He began marketing it accordingly, giving names to his models. He unleashed fireworks of new technology, new designs, new forms, new colors. The trailblazing spirit behind these remarkable instruments is the story of the brand, the story of Willy, and my story with Breitling."

**FRED MANDELBAUM**

*Breitling's brand historian is the author of* Premier Story: Breitling Premier, Duograph and Datora.

# 40

## RATTRAPANTE REVEAL

Breitling produced catalogs to advertise its growing stable of references. These product showcases were Willy Breitling's pride and joy. So much so, he sometimes couldn't resist sharing upcoming innovations that were still on the drawing board. One of his early reveals was the remarkable Duograph rattrapante proudly touted in the 1940 catalog. But bringing the complex chrono to life would prove no small feat. At the time, the only available industrialized split-second ebauches were designed for pocket timekeepers, and far too big for the elegant wristwatches Willy had in mind. Breitling and its movement maker Venus had to develop a whole new family of rattrapantes for case sizes of 36 and 38 mm. It would take another three years for the Duograph to finally hit the market, and when it did, Willy used the opportunity to poke fun at his tendency to jump the gun. The 1943 ad for the Duograph showed it playfully growing from the pages of the 1940 catalog.

*LEFT*
***An ad showing the Duograph growing out of the 1940 catalog was Willy's little joke***

BASE 1000
TÉLÉMÈTRE 1Km
Breitling

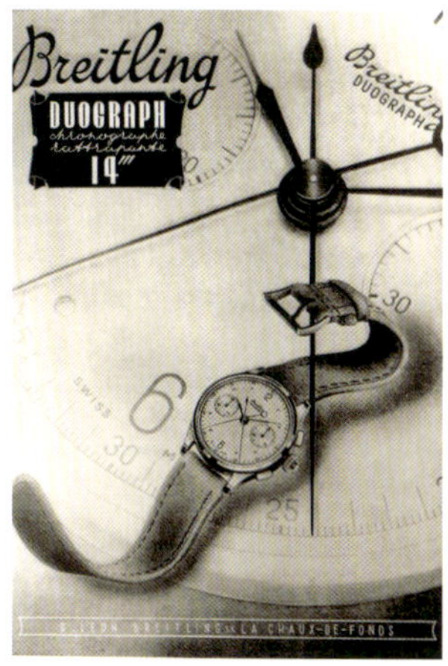


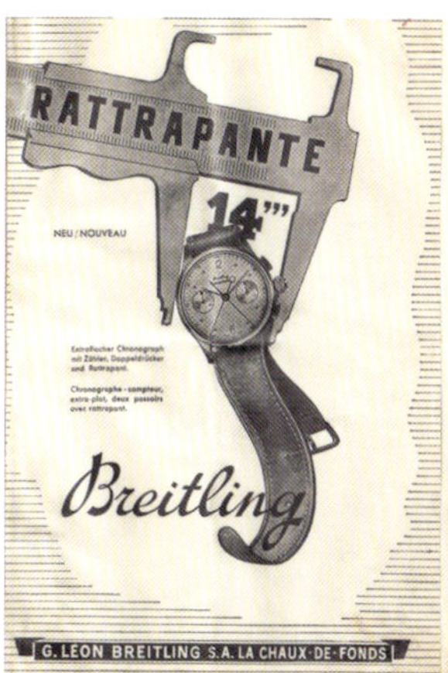

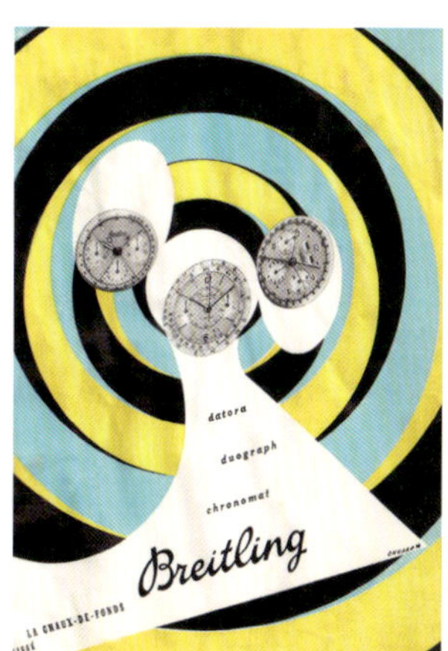


# 41

## PUBLICITY ON PARADE

Breitling's 1930s and '40s advertisements combined style with clever artistry. Straightforward promotion for brand novelties mingled alongside more esoteric messaging, like an image of a broom to denote an "out with the old, in with the new" approach to calibers, or a bottled chronograph implying that Breitling timekeepers were the remedy for business needs. Meanwhile, grand illustrations turned watch components into monumental icons impossible to miss.

19
32

# 42

19
79

1943

# DUOGRAPH 764

## RARE BEAST

The rattrapante split-second function had been a facet of Breitling pocket watches since 1891. Then in the 1940s, Willy Breitling decided to take the complication out of the pocket and onto the wrist. This early version, called a “doctor’s watch,” came in at an oversized [for the time] 38-millimeter diameter, was water-resistant, and featured a pulsometer dial. Surviving examples are hard to find. Breitling only ever produced 350 Duographs, including all references, from 1943 to 1970.

19
32

19
79

# 43

***"When a man puts on his watch, the world may see in this, his most treasured personal possession, the unmistakable stamp of impeccable taste."***

*WILLY BREITLING*

19
32

19
79

# 44

1947

# DATORA 799

## FULL CALENDAR CHRONO

Having mastered the wrist rattrapante, Willy Breitling enlisted his trusted movement maker, Venus, to add a second complication to his roster of elite chronographs: the full calendar. The Venus caliber 187 was the culmination of this effort. Breitling became one of the first brands to add calendar and moonphase functions to the chronograph—and the result is a watch that still wows today.

# 45

## ON TOUR WITH CYCLING'S BIGGEST NAMES

From 1936 to the mid-1950s, Willy Breitling developed a new category in his strategic marketing plan: sporting sponsorships, particularly cycling competitions. Breitling became the official timekeeper to the greatest races on the cycling calendar: the Tour de France, Milano-Sanremo, Fleche Wallonne, and Giro d'Italia. These thrilling endurance sports had become huge spectator events across Europe.

Willy amped up his brand recognition by going beyond sponsorship to leverage the star power of top athletes. It began with Fausto Coppi, the first racer to win both the Giro d'Italia and the Tour de France in the same year [in 1948 and again in 1952]. He later enlisted Coppi's great rival, Gino Bartali, nicknamed il Vecchio. These two athletes were mega-stars who caused a frenzy wherever they went, so kitting them out with Breitling watches was a marketing masterstroke. The strategic partnership with Giro d'Italia was the postwar equivalent of Breitling's association with the British War Office, another eureka moment, and the next logical step in Willy's pursuit of new markets for the chronograph.

During the time it was a sponsor of the race, Breitling produced annual Giro d'Italia limited editions, and they were showstoppers. Now rare collector's pieces, these chronographs epitomized Breitling's endeavor to infuse the mighty tool watch with elegance and glamour, taking it from the cockpit to the wrists of sporting gentlemen. The Giro d'Italia pieces were fine examples of the emerging luxury sports watch genre. They had solid-gold cases, applied golden numerals, guilloche dials, and hand designs that varied year to year, from lance to lumed lozenge. They were designated as ref. 1190 Giro d'Italia, and while it's difficult to pinpoint the exact number that were made, there is no question that they were quite limited.

The interesting thing about the ref. 1190 Giro d'Italia is that it was something of an outlier in the Premier line, the designated sports-luxury collection. It wasn't a Premier per se, because it was powered by the Venus 188 lever chronograph movement rather than the more sophisticated Venus 175 column-wheel caliber. But it was conceived as a showcase watch, and Willy felt that something defined as a "luxury sports" chronograph would be easier to achieve with the very flat and slim caliber 188.

Timing adventurous sporting events was a natural fit for the exuberant Willy Breitling, who often participated in the competitions he supported—which included gleefully driving ahead of the peloton in a Breitling-banner-draped cabriolet.

La Gazzetta dello Sport
GIRO D'ITALIA
Cronometraggio
OROLOGI
BREITLING
OROLOGI
BREITLING
GENEVE
SUISSE

THIS PAGE, CLOCKWISE FROM TOP LEFT
*Fausto Coppi receiving his watch from Breitling's Italian distributor, Benito Benaglio; riders Ferdi Kübler, Fausto Coppi, and Giancarlo Astrua in the Giro d'Italia; Willy Breitling and friends in the Breitling cabriolet; Benito Benaglio presents Gino Bartali with his watch*

OPPOSITE PAGE
*Route map publicity showing Breitling as the official chronograph of the Giro d'Italia*

Breitling
CRONOMETRO UFFICIALE
al giro d'Italia
La Gazzetta dello Sport
CRONOMETRO UFFICIALE Breitling
Breitling
CRONOMETRO UFFICIALE Breitling
La Gazzetta dello Sport
CRONOMETRO UFFICIALE Breitling
OROLOGI
Breitling
Breitling
OROLOGI Breitling
La Gazzetta dello Sport
ORGANIZZAZIONI
78

Breitling
DIVONNE

# 46

## WILLY'S GENEVA GAMBIT

In 1953 Willy Breitling relocated his headquarters from Rue Montbrillant in La Chaux-de-Fonds to Place du Molard in Geneva. The financial capital on Lac Leman was not only where most of the company's business transactions took place, it was also home to many of Breitling's competitors. Willy marked the move by adding "GENÈVE" to the company's dials, a privilege reserved for resident watchmakers.

1932
1979

# 47

# COMING TO AMERICA: THE BREITLING-WAKMANN PARTNERSHIP

*RIGHT*
*Breitling's U.S. distributor, Joseph Karasick, announcing the launch of the Chrono-matic, 1969*

How did Breitling navigate the turmoil of the 1940s and establish a global presence in the 1950s? It's a story of equal parts circumstance, chronograph, and *chutzpah*.

Switzerland was neutral during World War II, but for an adventurous watchmaker like Willy Breitling, selling cockpit clocks in wartime was still not without its risks. Willy was secretly delivering chronographs to the U.K.'s Royal Air Force, at night, on airstrips illuminated for the occasion by automobile headlamps. To have been caught could have cost him much more than his company.

Meanwhile, in what was neutral Portugal, Willy's friend and business associate Icko Wakmann was also covertly selling aircraft chronographs and pilot watches to the RAF. Icko's situation was even more precarious due to his Jewish roots. So much so that he insisted on an agreement with the Brits to fly him and his family to safety abroad if necessary. By 1942, that time had come.

Icko settled in New York City, where he set up shop on 5th Avenue and 40th Street and proceeded to establish what was then one of the largest U.S. watch brands, the Wakmann Watch Company. His genius was to import high-quality Swiss watch components, then complete their assembly in the United States, thereby skirting American tariff and country-of-origin rules.

The Breitling-Wakmann partnership grew as Icko made inroads in his adopted country. As his son-in-law, Joseph Karasick, who would later take over the Wakmann Watch Company, recalls, it took Icko, who knew little English, some time to get his bearings: "He spoke a bunch of languages, all in Yiddish!"

But Icko had a magnetic personality, and a brimming address book. He was only lacking in help. That help came in the late 1940s with Joseph, who had been a happily practicing rabbi in Montreal until Icko repeatedly *kvetched* to his reluctant son-in-law, "I'm all alone in business—I have no sons!"

Despite his early hesitation, Joseph proved a natural in the watch trade and quickly formed a strong bond with Willy: "He was *joie de vivre*, he was unbelievable. I was a youngster, but we became as close as brothers." And it was while sitting in Willy's office in Geneva that Joseph spotted a Breitling cockpit clock—a souvenir from the war. When he showed the clock to a Pan American pilot, it led to a redesign for use in commercial jets, and Breitling was suddenly a big part, not only of the American watch trade, but of the dawn of civil aviation.

Happenstance would play a part in the Breitling-Wakmann partnership once again. The relationship had given Icko and Joseph access to a little-known invention that would soon become very much in demand: the Navitimer. In 1952, the Aircraft Owners and Pilots Association (AOPA) approached Wakmann for a watch for its members. Joseph and Icko pitched them on Willy's revolutionary chronograph with a circular slide rule that would serve as "an onboard computer."

It was a historic moment. The association had found its official timepiece. The AOPA had it emblazoned with its name and winged logo. With that watch, worn by pilots the world over, Breitling became "the official supplier to world aviation."

By 1955, the Navitimer would receive a Breitling signature and be sold in the thousands, not just to AOPA members but to a growing fan base of corporate and individual clients. Through a friendship forged over decades, an icon was made.

19
32

19
79

# 48

1952

# BREITLING NAVITIMER MARK 1.1

## BIRTH OF AN ICON

In the 1950s, pilots depended on a circular slide rule to calculate everything from fuel consumption to rate of climb. So when Willy Breitling added one to the rotating bezel of a chronograph, he created a flight computer like no other. The name said it all—a combination of "navigation" and "timer." A prelaunch of 100 pieces in 1954 followed two years of development with the Aircraft Owners and Pilots Association (AOPA). Breitling was en route to becoming the "official supplier to world aviation."

# 49

## NAVITIMER DESIGN EVOLUTION

1955
### NAVITIMER 806 MARK 2.1
AOPA members are snapping up their official watch, and its movement gets an upgrade to the Venus 178 for enhanced reliability. With its popularity growing beyond aviation, the Navitimer goes on general sale, now with Breitling on its dial.

1963
### NAVITIMER 806 MARK 3
The look that will endure: easy to read white-on-black "reverse panda" subdials, slimmer hands, baton-index hour markers, and a new arrow-tipped sweep hand. The iconic signature of an all-time classic is almost complete.

1964
### NAVITIMER 806 MARK 5
Say goodbye to the rice beads on the rotating bezel and hello to easy-grip notches. Civil aviation is officially in its heyday, and the Navitimer will have a Twin Jet logo within a year. AOPA members, though, keep their coveted wings.

1973
### NAVITIMER CHRONO-MATIC 8806
Breitling's collaboration to create the self-winding chrono results in an automatic movement in the classic Navi case. The caliber 12 crown is on the left, and there are only two subdials, but this is progress.

2003

2010

2022

1980

### NAVITIMER JUPITER QUARTZ 80970

Businessman and pilot Ernest Schneider is newly at the controls of Breitling, and quartz is the only game in town. Ads boast two time zones, water resistance, and a five-year guarantee.

2003

### NAVITIMER CHRONOMETRE

A refocus on 1950s aviation elegance by Ernest's son, Theodore. The case has grown to 41.8 mm, but a fifties' pilot would love the return of the 3-6-9 subdials. Oh, and every Breitling watch is now a COSC-certified chronometer.

2010

### NAVITIMER 01 LIMITED EDITION

The tool watch elevated. It's no wonder the winged logo catches the light: it's made of white gold. A red date display defines the dial, while a transparent caseback shows off the new Breitling Manufacture Caliber 01.

2022

### NAVITIMER B01 CHRONOGRAPH 43

All the classic features with a modern twist, 70 years on from the first Navitimer drawings, CEO Georges Kern makes it a birthday to remember. It's colorful, impeccably styled, and instantly recognizable.

19
32

19
79

# 50

## NAVITIMER B19 CHRONOGRAPH 43 140TH ANNIVERSARY

A watchmaker with a history as celebrated as Breitling's has had many firsts in its catalog, but the Navitimer B19 Chronograph 43 Perpetual Calendar 140th Anniversary is a superlative among them. Reflecting the Navitimer's role in the heyday of commercial aviation, Breitling harnessed the new caliber B19 to introduce the ultimate complication, a perpetual calendar. Like all the 140-year editions, an open caseback displays the movement alongside Leon Breitling's Rue de Montbrillant factory on its solid gold rotor.

BREITLING
1884
MPH KM
SWISS
MADE

19
32

19
79

# 51

## MILES DAVIS: SARTORIAL SOUNDS

Defined by Bob Dylan as the very definition of cool, Miles Davis paired a smooth trumpet sound with a magnetic presence that captivated audiences. Beyond his jazz mastery, he was a cultural icon with a penchant for luxury that included sharp Italian suits and a fleet of exotic sports cars. His accessory of choice, a Navitimer Mark 5, remained an onstage fixture throughout his career, a reflection of his enduring style.

1932

# 52

1979

## 1953
# 765 AVI MARK I DIGITAL
### CO-PILOT FOR LIFE

There's no room for error in a cockpit, so pilots in the 1950s may have been torn in their choice of timepiece. Go with the Navitimer for its computational slide rule or the AVI for pure legibility. This unique tool watch could not be clearer. What looks like a date window at three o'clock is a digital 15-minute totalizer. Press the top pusher and the number changes every 60 seconds. With reliability derived from Breitling's decades of flight-tool experience, this is a chronograph that deserves to take its name from aviation.

19
32

19
79

# 53

## CLASSIC AVI
## DESIGN EVOLUTION

1959
### 765 AVI MARK 1 ANALOG

Same functionality as the digital version but with a different tack. An enlarged 15-minute counter is easy to read and marked in threes for rapid calculations. It predates so many imitators, collectors will call it "Lucy," after one of the earliest humans.

1963
### 765 AVI MARK 2

It's on the market for four years when a silver-screen cameo propels the AVI to stardom. When Raquel Welch wears one in *Fathom*, Breitling ads featuring the film's star declare: "For today's young people, enjoyment means excitement."

1965
### 765 AVI MARK 3

The bezel is anodized for improved legibility of the timer function, and it gets the suffix "CP" for "Co-Pilot." The enlarged minute counter still stands out, as will skier Jean-Claude Killy, wearing it as he wins three Olympic golds in 1968.

1969
### 7650 AVI YACHTING

Swinging Sixties' flair is reflected in a wider bezel—at an impressive 42.8 mm—and splashes of nautical color. Designed for the complex countdowns at the start of regattas, it underlines Breitling's commitment to air, land, and sea.

1996

### AVIASTAR

AVI production was dropped when watchmaking hit hard times in the quartz crisis, but this model brings it back. The Valjoux 7750 moves the subdials to 6-9-12, but the HUIT-inspired high-contrast markings, syringe hands, and slim bezel are all there.

2021

### SUPER AVI CHRONOGRAPH GMT 46 MOSQUITO

With its ceramic bezel and strap stitching styled after vintage flight gear, this AVI pays homage to the plane known as "The Wooden Wonder." The red-tipped GMT hand adds interest, while an open caseback shows off the caliber.

2023

### CLASSIC AVI CHRONOGRAPH 42 P-51 MUSTANG

The aircraft tribute series is back in a scaled-down 42-mm format. This execution is a tribute to the famous American fighter aircraft. Fun fact: the dial contains the "hidden" map coordinates of the Breitling Chronometrie.

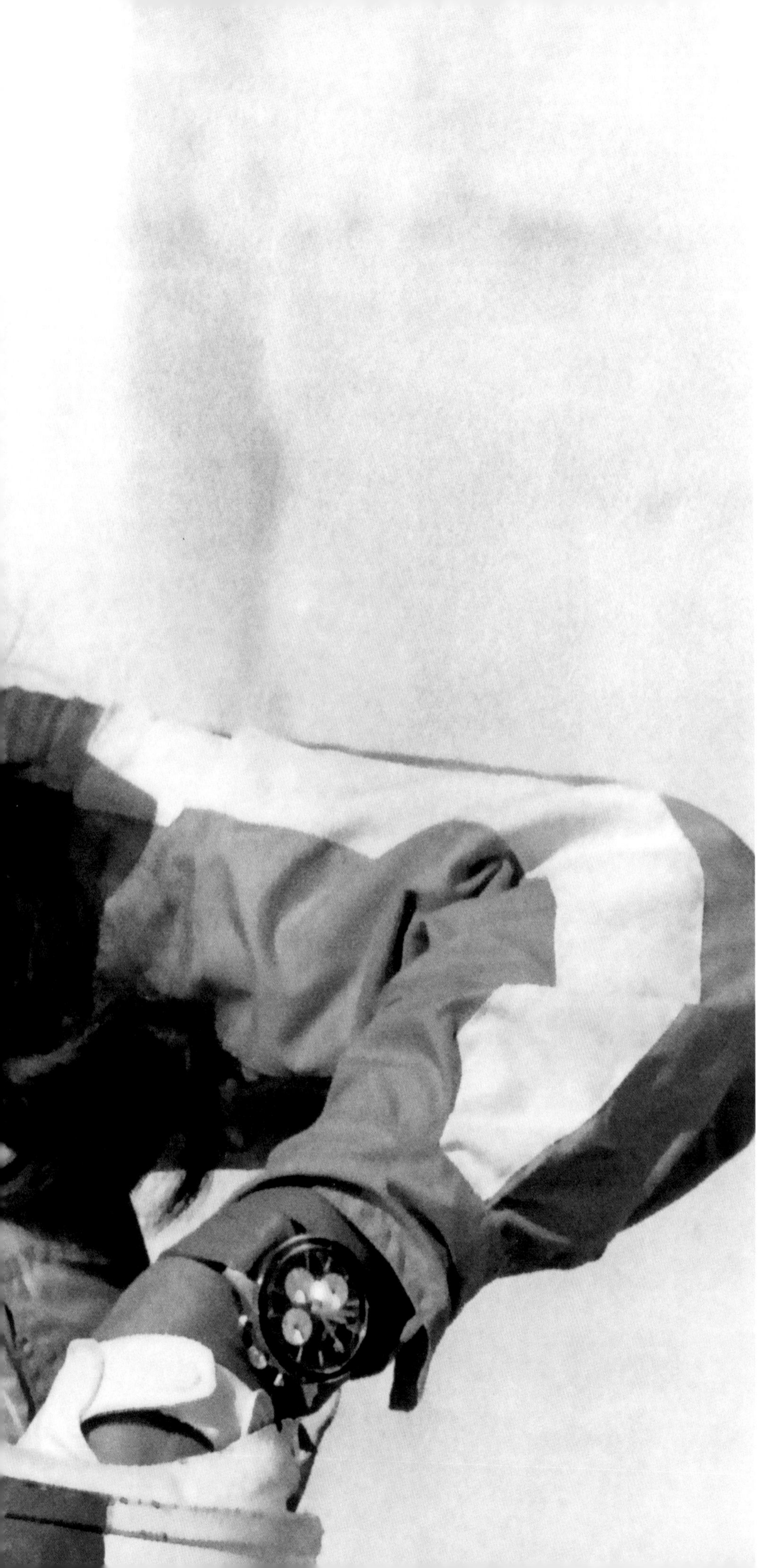

# 54

## RAQUEL WELCH: FATHOM'S FLIGHT

A wristwatch may not be the first thing one notices when the wondrous Raquel Welch takes to the screen, but in the 1967 spy thriller *Fathom*, she sports Breitling's rugged aviator chronograph, the AVI ref. 765 Co-Pilot. Her character, skydiver Fathom Harvill, is on a mission to recover an atomic-bomb device. In the campy Cold War epic, she ultimately prevails, and demonstrates to a generation that not only do women make formidable action heroes, they can also pull off a kick-ass chrono.

# 55

## SAY HELLO TO YELLOW

We don't know for certain if yellow was Willy Breitling's favorite color, but in 1957 he and the company's marketing mastermind, Georges Caspari, decided to use it for all aspects of Breitling brand communications. Henceforth it would be seen in everything from store windows to manuals, badges, stickers, bags, and boxes. Willy unveiled the whole rollout plan in an internal document labeled "Top Secret" that was appropriately printed on yellow paper. When dissent arose—"too bright," "too flashy"—Willy reminded his staff that in the mostly black-and-white publications of the day, Breitling's yellow ads would be impossible to miss. Once again Willy was ahead of the times, foreseeing that a brand identity depended on a consistent image. The introduction of the corporate color was timed to coincide with the launch of Breitling's first dive watch, the SuperOcean, and its "traveling man's" companion, the TransOcean. The company has never abandoned the yellow concept. More than four decades later, Breitling's then-head of marketing, Ben Balmer, would sum it up when he delivered his own internal communiqué, saying: "We all need to have the same blood in our veins. Yellow blood."

# 56

## TWIN JET LOGO

As another element of the corporate repositioning, when Willy Breitling was beginning to conceive of Breitling as a "brand," 1957 also saw the birth of the Twin Jet logo. But you had to go looking for it, either on the caseback of the SuperOcean and TransOcean, or on point-of-sale documents. However, by 1965 Willy was ready to bring it to the Navitimer dial. This striking image of superimposed jets has continued to crop up on special-edition Navitimers over the years and appears on current models as an if-you-know-you-know caseback engraving. Why two jets? There seems to be no record of that, but the duo is certainly graphically dynamic.

# 57

## TIMING IN THE DEEP

In 1943 Jacques Cousteau, a French naval officer, explorer, and conservationist, and Emile Gagnan, a French engineer, co-invented their famous "aqualung," a contraption that made it possible to breathe underwater. Cousteau's invention, along with his mesmerizing below-the-waves documentaries, would inspire the postwar generation to take up diving as a leisure activity. Underwater, timing was of the essence. That's where the need for precision dive watches came in. It was a new depth Breitling would soon chart for itself.

19
32

19
79

# 58

1957

# SUPEROCEAN 1004

## MORE THAN SURFACE BEAUTY

In 1956, Jacques Cousteau and Louis Malle's *The Silent World* took the Palme d'Or at Cannes, setting off a tidal wave of interest in underwater adventures. Capturing the moment, Breitling unveiled a dive watch with a concave bezel, bold hour markers, and a sleek silhouette that proved as mesmerizing on sandy shores as it was indispensable in the ocean's depths. From then on, sea joined air and land as a Breitling "universe."

19
32

19
79

# 59

## SUPEROCEAN HERITAGE DESIGN EVOLUTION

1957
### SUPEROCEAN 1004

This mint-condition three-hand belonged to Willy Breitling's wife, Beatrice. Together with the 807 chronograph, the models made a "his and hers" duo, tailored to the sports set. The clean lines and crisp contrasts were a statement of mid-century modernity.

1957
### SUPEROCEAN 807

The 1004's chronograph counterpart earns its place in watchmaking history with the first white-on-black "reverse panda" subdials. They make the 30-minute recorder easy to read underwater, while the mesh bracelet enhances its 1950s leisure style.

2007
### SUPEROCEAN HERITAGE 46

To mark the 50th anniversary of the first SuperOcean, the line makes a twenty-first-century comeback. While resembling the ref. 1004, the Superocean Heritage has grown to 46 mm and offers a ratcheted dive bezel and glare-protected crystal.

2012
### SUPEROCEAN HERITAGE 44

Drawing on the best of Breitling's dive-watch past, the first SuperOcean Heritage chronograph deserves its name. The twin subdials and striking good looks are inherited from 1957's ref. 807 with its beach-culture wearability.

2017
## SUPEROCEAN HERITAGE II 42 B20

For its 60th anniversary, the Superocean Heritage receives a design refresh and a power upgrade. The manufacture caliber B20 powers subtler hands, and the ratcheted dive bezel is now made of ceramic.

2018
## SUPEROCEAN HERITAGE II B01

The Breitling Manufacture Caliber 01 gives a 70-hour power reserve, and a scratch-resistant ceramic bezel adds to its dressy look. From the hands and logos to the mesh strap, the original design elements have worn well.

2020
## SUPEROCEAN HERITAGE 57

The "57" in its name says it all. This iteration of the Superocean Heritage features two signature elements of the original ref. 1004: a concave bidirectional ceramic bezel and a dial featuring its signature oversized art-deco-style indices.

# 60

## THE LIFE AQUATIC

Willy and Beatrice Breitling enjoy a family barbecue at their summer home on Lake Geneva. She is wearing the SuperOcean ref. 1004, Breitling's first dive watch, and Willy wears the chronograph version, ref. 807. According to family lore, Willy had a little too much wine that day and burnt the chicken skewers. Fortunately, an after-dinner plunge in the lake posed no danger to his dive watch.

19
32

19
79

# 61

BREITLING
GENEVE
SuperOcean
SWISS MADE T
50
10
15
20
30
40
45
30

1964

# SUPEROCEAN 2005 MARK I

## A CHRONO WITHOUT A SECONDS HAND

Dubbed the "Slow-Motion," the ref. 2005 baffled many with its chrono hand timing minutes, not seconds, essential for divers to monitor submersion and decompression. Its minute-centric design improved legibility for underwater reading. The timer was subtle, ticking over every 60 seconds. To confirm operation, Breitling added a six o'clock activity indicator [aka "the dot"] to show when the hand was engaged, paused, or off, ensuring divers could see its status at a glance.

62

# SUPEROCEAN
# DESIGN EVOLUTION

1970
### SUPEROCEAN 2005 MK. 2
The Slow-Motion chronograph is upgraded with a new, exclusive movement manufactured by Valjoux, adding running seconds at nine o'clock. Hands are even more of a focal point, the "paddle" minute counter giving it unmistakable character.

1970
### SUPEROCEAN 2105 CHRONO-MATIC
The "Pizza" SuperOcean, powered by the first automatic dive chronograph (cal. 12) and certified to 200 m. In 1970s style, it is colorful and huge, at a diameter of 48 mm, but still surprisingly comfortable to wear.

1995
### COLT SUPEROCEAN
Fifties' beach style gives way to U.S. Navy SEAL specifications. There's a nod to the paddle hand, but the glass can withstand one-ton pressures, and a decompression valve prevents it from exploding, even after a 1,000 m dive.

2006
### SUPEROCEAN STEELFISH
The name comes from Theodore Schneider's love of the "striking and provocative," and he's increased the water resistance to 1,500 m. Wide hands, a high contrast dial, and oversized hour markers are all taken from the SuperOcean back catalog.

2015
**SUPEROCEAN II 44**

A new generation of the fully loaded diver's watch with oversized numerals for enhanced legibility. In the same vein, the bezel has a bold 15-minute timeout scale and a luminous circle in the signature triangle at 12 o'clock.

2022
**SUPEROCEAN AUTOMATIC 42**

Standout colors give a modern look to a design based on the retro Slow Motion, with paddle hands and a nod to "the dot." Water-resistant to 300 m, it shakes off sand and seawater, and can take a beating in the surf.

2022
**SUPEROCEAN AUTOMATIC 46**

The bidirectional scratchproof ceramic-inlayed bezel is designed to never wear or fade. For safety, it is equipped with a patented lock. This is no longer strictly a dive watch—surf with it, swim with it, hit the beach bar with it.

# 63

## BRAND CRAFT

Willy Breitling was determined that Breitling be more than the sum of its products and points of sale. He was building a brand at a time when the concept of corporate identity was still in its infancy, a direction he emphasized in a 1957 repositioning document for distributors: "The very fact that you are selling a brand and not 'unestablished' watches gives our business collaboration a certain standing from the start. It is fundamentally the collaboration of two outlooks, and the basis of this collaboration is respect for the brand."

# 64 LUNAR INSPIRATION: BREITLING'S TRIBUTE TO THE SPACE AGE

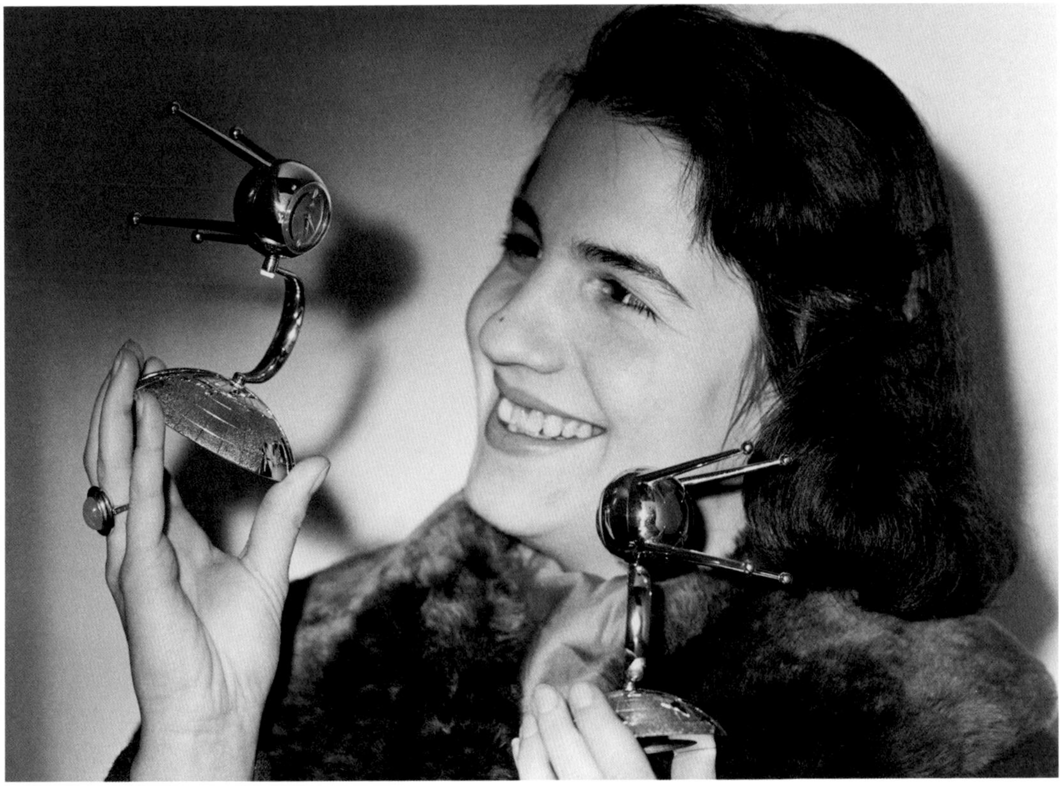

"My father was passionate about everything that involved flying. In the early days of space travel, Willy was there, soaking everything up. He was overjoyed when, on October 4, 1957, he heard the first beeps from the Russian satellite Sputnik over the radio. When it launched, we were at our summer house on Lake Geneva. The sky was clear, no clouds. We got out our telescope and went into the back yard to watch for it. We were looking around like crazy and finally saw a point of light in the sky moving very fast. It was Sputnik.

To mark the occasion, Willy created a table clock he called Bébé Lune—or Baby Moon—a reference to how the satellite looked to us in the sky that night. The table clock predated by five years what would be Willy's ultimate tribute to space travel: the Navitimer Cosmonaute, a watch that orbited the Earth, becoming the first Swiss wristwatch to do so. Many people have asked why he called it the Cosmonaute, which was the Russian name for a space pilot. It seemed like taking sides when the Americans and Russians were in the midst of a heated space race. In truth, the decision was practical: the American name *Astronaut* was already taken by another watch company. Other options were the French *Spationaute* or Chinese *Taikonaut*, but none had quite the same ring. Thankfully, the watch was still called the Navitimer when NASA astronaut Scott Carpenter wore it into space. If it hadn't, I'm not sure he would have taken it. But the name—and the watch—caught on nonetheless, becoming a symbol of the early space age."

**GREGORY BREITLING**

*The eldest son of Willy Breitling grew up surrounded by his father's watchmaking influences and today is the official spokesperson for the Breitling family.*

# 65

# FLIGHT OF THE COSMONAUTE: A WRISTWATCH IN SPACE

*RIGHT*
*Clockwise from top: the original 1962 Cosmonaute, showing its extraterrestrial appearance; an intact Cosmonaute from the era; and a 60th-anniversary limited re-edition*

In 1962 it wasn't common for a watch brand to accept a cold call from a customer wanting a one-off timepiece. But when Willy Breitling received such a request from a man from Langley Air Force Base, Virginia, he found the pitch impossible to turn down.

The caller was Scott Carpenter, one of the Mercury 7 group of pioneering NASA astronauts. Carpenter was in charge of the Mercury capsule's onboard navigational equipment, with the astronauts' watches being within his area of responsibility. Early into his training, he'd seen Royal Australian Air Force pilots using the slide rule on their Breitling Navitimer chronographs to carry out flight calculations.

The watch didn't just appeal to Carpenter's pilot sensibilities, but to his desire to return to Earth in one piece. As his daughter Kris Stoever remarked at a Breitling event on the 60th anniversary of his space flight, "The important thing for him was to be prepared at all times and to train for disaster, to train and then train some more, and to have every piece of equipment that you needed for an emergency." He saw the Navitimer as just such a tool.

To optimize the Navitimer for use in space, Carpenter requested three changes. First, because he would be circumnavigating the planet once every 90 minutes, he would require a 24-hour dial, rather than the usual 12 hours. With this, he could keep his watch on UTC, and instantly know the time at mission control. Second, he asked that a dial scale used for calculations that weren't useful in space be removed to improve legibility. Finally, he requested that the rotating bezel be made wider for better grip in his thick astronaut's gloves.

As a longtime space enthusiast, Willy Breitling was thrilled that Carpenter had selected a Navitimer and made the changes as quickly as possible. The astronaut received his special watch a few days before the flight, and on May 24, 1962, Carpenter's modified Navitimer became the first Swiss wristwatch in space.

A mechanical problem with the automatic stabilization and control system caused the astronaut to overshoot his designated landing area by 250 nautical miles. After splashdown, he spent three hours in a small life raft awaiting rescue. Carpenter's water-logged watch stopped running soon after he was plucked from the sea.

With Carpenter's modifications in place, the Navitimer went into production as the Cosmonaute. Scott Carpenter returned the model he wore on May 24, 1962 to Breitling, and Willy promptly replaced it with a new one. The original was not seen by the public until 2022, when it was revealed by Willy's son Gregory on the 60th anniversary of Carpenter's flight. Incredibly, the watch's hands were stopped exactly where Carpenter had last seen them and the seawater had distorted the dial, giving it an otherworldly appearance—fittingly so, given its incredible journey.

Weltrau
osmonau
Uhr hat den a
ommander Sco
s2 erfolgreich bes
Mod. 809
Ausführung
stellbarem Ed
Zifferblatt mit 2
Einteilung.
BREITLING
NAVITIMER
NAVITIMER

*TOP*
*Scott Carpenter wearing his Cosmonaute (right) with fellow astronaut John Glenn*

*ABOVE*
*Carpenter in a training exercise for the ocean landings NASA anticipated*

*RIGHT*
*Carpenter inspecting the cabin of Aurora 7 prior to ingress*

7
AURORA

# BREITL

Breitling Watches – 6 Place du Molard, G

## in the air

**Navitimer**

17 jewel exclusive chronograph, calibrated with logarithmic scales of an aerial navigation computer. Movable bezel; 12-hour recorder; 30-minute register; luminous dial. Stainless steel, gold filled or 18 ct. gold.
from Sw. Fr. 295
to Sw. Fr. 630

## on the grounc

**Chronomat**

17 jewel exclusive slid
rule chronograph; solve
complicated mathematic
al and engineering pro
blems: multiplication, d
vision, ratios, interes
percentages,speeds,ave
ages, etc. Stainless stee
gold filled or 18 ct. gold.
from Sw. Fr. 250
to Sw. Fr. 590

## why not on your wrist?

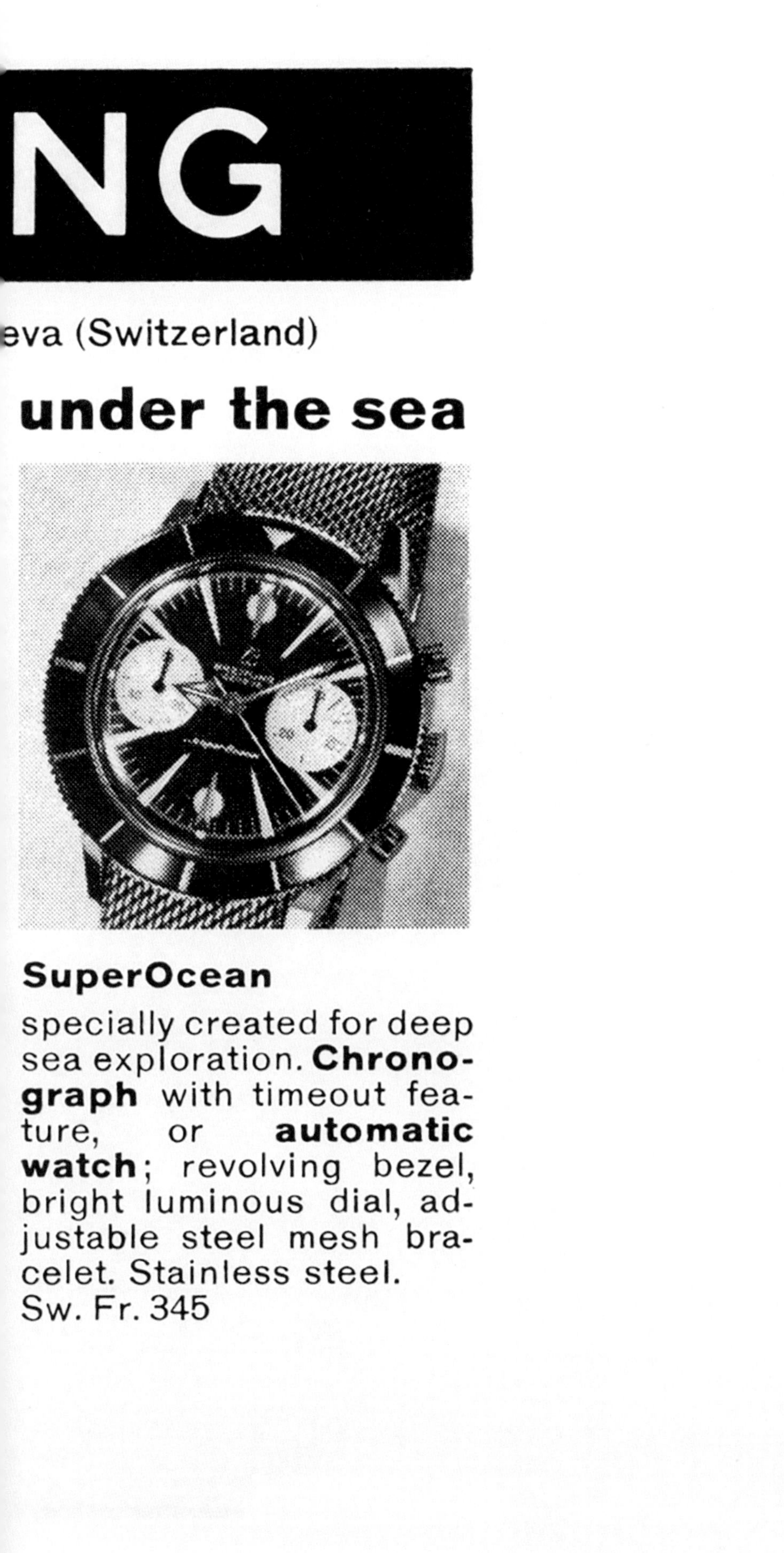


# 66

## AIR LAND SEA

Willy Breitling set out to conquer the world with his chronographs, and with the popularity of his newly launched dive watches, he had succeeded. Willy could now lay claim to the fact that Breitling's precision timepieces were hard at work "in the air, on the ground, and under the sea"—a concept that would make a comeback at Breitling more than half a century later.

# 67
# TOP TIME: MAKING THE CHRONOGRAPH COOL AGAIN

*RIGHT*
***Ad evoking the Top Time's dial designs***

Ever seen the oceangoing documentary *The Silent World*, by Jacques Cousteau and Louis Malle? If so, it may have made you want to drop what you were doing, join the crew of the *Calypso*, and start exploring the underwater world. And you wouldn't have been alone. Suddenly diving—and dive watches—were all the rage. That was 1956.

This did not bode well for Willy Breitling as a maker of chronographs. Sales of his watches were diving too—nosediving, that is. The zeitgeist had changed, and Willy could feel it. The world he was living in was all about youth, a demographic that saw the chrono as a relic of wartime. It was their father's watch.

Willy's response was a two-pronged attack. One was easy enough: he addressed the diving craze by introducing the water-resistant SuperOcean and TransOcean. But reaching the youth market would prove an entirely different affair.

For starters, he didn't want to rely on intuition alone. So in his typically thorough fashion, he became president of the Association of Chronograph Manufacturers [part of the Federation of the Swiss Watch Industry] and commissioned a study to pinpoint the problem. It indeed revealed that Swiss watchmakers needed to target youth. Breitling's marketing guru Georges Caspari designed a series of ads exhorting Swiss watchmakers to get out of their wartime chronograph doldrums and cater to the new generation. Using the term "teenage" as shorthand for anyone under 30, his take was that, "In the teenager world, chronographs stand for achievement" and, in a subsequent ad for Breitling, that "Pop's watchmaker is out of tune."

"Teenagers today have a language of their own. Just listen to them talking," said Caspari in a 1963 trade-magazine interview. "The young have swift reactions, a taste for science-fiction and spend money quickly. They need to obtain as much as possible in the minimum time." He could still work in advertising today.

What was Willy's response to the changing times? He realized that merely repositioning the tool-watch chronograph, as he had successfully done with the elegant Premier line, was no longer enough. His answer was the Top Time, a chrono so fresh and different from its predecessors that it became a hit in the 1960s.

It not only met the need to measure speed, with readings to one-fifth of a second, it also set fashion trends with its graphic dial designs and square "cushion-case" variants. What's more, it had a unisex appeal that fit in with the burgeoning women's liberation movement, a bold departure from—as one Top Time ad put it—the "fussily feminine watches of yesteryear."

Sales once again soared, and Willy's systematic approach not only ensured the continued relevance of the chronograph, but represented a personal triumph. He had tapped into the verve of the era and put the chrono back in style.

# OP ART BY BREITLING

ABOVE
*The cover of a study into declining chronograph sales urges watchmakers to go after youth*

LEFT
*Top Time models with graphic dials and cushion cases*

RIGHT
*Men and women were equally drawn to the Top Time*

JEAN
MURIT
BP

19
32

19
79

# 68

1967

# TOP TIME 810 MARK 2

## THE UNCONVENTIONAL CHRONOGRAPH

A new generation is on the march, and Willy Breitling is a step ahead. His bold and graphic revision of the chrono is "a competition watch with special dials... impressive and really elegant." The Beatles are singing "I Am the Walrus," and Breitling's competitors are shaking their heads, but a watch with a name as catchy as the Fab Four grabs all the attention. The chronograph for "young and active professionals" has captured a new market and never looks back.

# 69

## TOP TIME
## DESIGN EVOLUTION

1964
### TOP TIME 810 MARK 1

Chiming with youth culture, it's a reliable chronograph with a traditionally slim profile and a wide-for-the-day 38-millimeter width. There are three dial options, and it's so precise, one ad declares that "it splits life's every precious second into fifths!"

1964
### TOP TIME 2002

When James Bond needs a Geiger counter in *Thunderball*, Q has the perfect solution: a modified Top Time. Would-be spies can wear the instantly recognizable original while practicing Sean Connery's trademark raised eyebrow.

1965
### TOP TIME 2008

The experimental decade sees "the cushion"—a shape between a square and a circle—pop up in art, fabrics, and even roundabouts. The fashionable set is won over by ads describing the cushion-case Top Time as "daringly different."

1972
### TOP TIME LONG PLAYING 815

Taking its name from the LPs in everyone's album collection, it's the perfect description for the watch's 12-hour recorder and 52-hour power reserve. A mesmerizing ice-blue dial is the bonus track that will be re-released 50 years later.

2023

### TOP TIME B01 SHELBY COBRA

Back with a powerful new engine, the Top Time Classic Cars collection (first released in 2021) is updated with the Breitling Manufacture Caliber 01. Twin subdials and a high-octane 1960s motor racing vibe: What's not to like?

2023

### TOP TIME B01 DEUS

In partnership with Australian surf-and-motorcycle brand Deus Ex Machina, the black-and-white reverse panda returns. Three counters, those distinctive mushroom pushers, and a dash of color let the sports chronograph live on in style.

2023

### TOP TIME B01 TRIUMPH

Breitling and Triumph Motorcycles are a match made in heaven. The ice-blue 1970s Top Time Long Playing is a shade away from Marlon Brando's '50s Thunderbird in *The Wild One*. Together on a brushed dial they are the colors of ice itself.

2023

### TOP TIME B01

The ultimate expression of Willy Breitling's inspiration: impressive, elegant—and in solid 18 k red gold. Its clean look lets you appreciate the squircle subdials and perforated racing strap. The freewheeling 1960s vibe has never looked so good.

# 70

## PROJECT 99: THE RACE TO MAKE THE AUTOMATIC CHRONOGRAPH

*RIGHT*
*Chrono-matic reveal in Geneva. From left: Robert Kocher (Hamilton Buren), Gerald Dubois (Dubois-Depraz), Gerard Bauer (Swiss Watchmakers Association), Georges Caspari (Breitling's marketing director), Jack Heuer (Heuer Leonidas), Willy Breitling*

In the Swinging Sixties, the Swiss watch scene was abuzz with two distinct trends: sleek, sporty chronographs and increasingly popular automatic watches, nudging out their manually wound counterparts. But as yet, no one had succeeded in merging the two. Breitling and its Swiss peers knew that to combine these two technologies was a ticket to market dominance. The race was on to launch the first automatic chronograph.

Creating this horological hybrid, though, was no easy feat. It was a complex puzzle that either financially or technically few watch companies were willing to undertake alone. So in 1966, Breitling teamed up with some unlikely allies—rivals Heuer Leonidas and Hamilton Buren, plus the savvy component maker Dubois-Depraz—to brainstorm this breakthrough.

Each brought a strength to the table, creating a synergy that turned competitors into collaborators. Breitling and Heuer were the chronograph experts. Hamilton Buren, the specialist in automatic watches that had been perfecting the micro-rotors ideal for this venture. And Dubois-Depraz? They were the ace up the sleeve, experts in crafting complex modular movements.

Dubbed "Project 99," this secret mission was a race against time and external competition. Rather than developing a more time-consuming integrated caliber, the collaborators took a modular approach, equipping a Hamilton Buren automatic base with a newly designed Dubois-Depraz chronograph module. This innovative "Chrono-matic" movement featured a novel layout: hour recorder at nine o'clock, minute recorder at three, and a date window at six, all encased in a design that placed the crown distinctively on the left.

On March 3, 1969, the world met the Chrono-matic in simultaneous press conferences in Geneva and New York. While competitors had been hot on their trail—with one Swiss company showcasing a prototype earlier that year and a Japanese brand launching locally—Breitling, Heuer, and Hamilton were the first to bring automatic chronographs to a global audience in the summer of 1969. The alliance each presented their unique take on the design, with Breitling offering five different case styles, including the memorable "pizza."

In line with the transformative spirit of the 1960s, the automatic chronograph marked a significant milestone in horology—a daring leap of Swiss ingenuity that remains the most popular style of chronograph to this day.

HÔTEL
INTERCONTINENTAL
GENEVE

*THIS PAGE, CLOCKWISE FROM TOP*
*A SuperOcean from 1969 containing the new automatic chronograph caliber; component diagram for the Chrono-matic; French ad stating that "Breitling has solved the problem" of how to combine an automatic watch with a chronograph*

*OPPOSITE PAGE*
*Another ad refers to the Chrono-matic as "one watch inside another," urging readers to "Do the impossible!"*

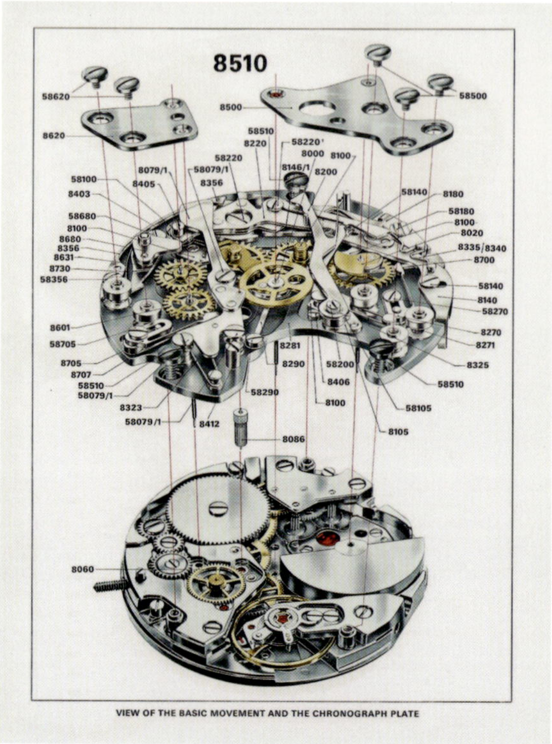

# DO THE IMPOSSIBLE!

# WEAR ONE WATCH INSIDE ANOTHER!

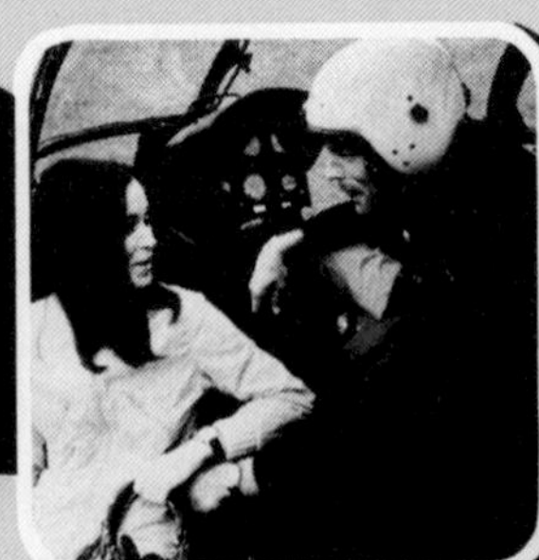

Until now you had to choose. Either you sported a chronograph, the watch with a built-in brain. Or you opted for the convenience of a self-winding watch. No single timepiece combined the advantages of both. Until Breitling invented the CHRONO-MATIC.

The CHRONO-MATIC is, in effect, a miniature computer, ready to reckon the most complex calculations. Instantaneously To an accuracy of fifths of seconds! But it is also a self-winding watch, complete with calendar on its dashing, instrument-panel dial. So the CHRONO-MATIC is really two watches in one.

2112
CHRONO-MATIC
Self-winding
Waterproof
Calendar
<

1806 steel
NAVITIMER
Self-winding
Waterproof
Calendar >

CHRONO-MATIC

The greatest watchmaking invention for years — and years to come.

Please send me, free of charge, your new catalogue in full colour — a real encyclopaedia of the most modern and versatile chronographs yet designed!

Name: Christian name:
Profession:
Address:
Town: Country:

G. Léon Breitling S.A., rue Adrien Lachenal 26, Genève, Suisse

BREITLING
GENEVA

19
32

19
79

# 71

1969

# CHRONO-MATIC 2110

## A CLASSIC ON THE CUTTING EDGE

In 1969 Breitling unveiled this bold addition to the nascent world of automatic chronographs. Its design married innovation with a touch of tradition, housing the avant-garde Chrono-matic caliber 11 in a classic round case with sharp lugs and a rotating bezel. The dial popped, with red and orange hands against a stark white backdrop, complemented by black subdials. At 40 mm, its oversized look was right at home going into the style-statement 1970s.

# 72

## WE DID THAT
# THE PIZZA

Breitling had successfully sent its Cosmonaute wristwatch into space, but that same watch was destroyed by seawater when the capsule splashed down in the Atlantic. A dismayed Willy Breitling set out to improve the water resistance of his slide-rule cases and, in 1966, enlisted the help of Ervin Piquerez, a specialist in dive-watch designs. The collaboration resulted in a case with a gear-driven bezel housed both under and around the crystal, giving the watch a phenomenal water resistance of 200 meters. The only catch: to accommodate its mechanics, this case had to be big—48 millimeters big—a size almost unheard-of for the time. Lauded for its engineering, the design would go on to house SuperOcean, AVI, Chronomat, GMT, and Navitimer models, but its most enduring claim to fame would be its nickname: "The Pizza."

19
32

19
79

# 73

1972

# SPRINT REF. 2016

## 70S DAY GLO

This Breitling Sprint can't hide its 1970s roots, but it is truly when worn that it shows its best asset: its weight. A resin case makes it incredibly light; it was intended for athletes, which also explains the heart-rate scale on the bezel. The featherlight case and eye-catching colors will go on to influence a modern Breitling athletic line, the Endurance Pro.

19
32

19
79

# 74
# QUARTZ CRISIS: A CHRONOLOGY OF CHALLENGES

*RIGHT*
*Swiss watch industry workers demand protection for their jobs, 1982*

In the 1970s, horology faced a seismic shift. Inexpensive quartz watches flooded the market and the Swiss watchmaking industry couldn't compete with their price or accuracy. But the era dubbed the "Quartz Crisis" wasn't only about new technology. A series of factors combined to create a disastrous decade for the Swiss watch industry.

Rewind to World War II, where neutral Switzerland was ticking along untouched by the war's devastation. Unlike many of their European counterparts, Swiss watchmaking factories didn't have to switch to wartime production, allowing the industry to thrive uninterrupted. In fact, from 1935 to 1945, Swiss watch catalogs flourished, showcasing innovations like new chronograph movements and complications. By the end of the war, Swiss watchmakers had smoothly transitioned from pocket watches to the wristwatches that would define the century.

At the Bretton Woods conference in 1944, global economic gears shifted. This new system, set up to aid war-torn economies, unexpectedly handed Switzerland a golden ticket. The fixed exchange rates pegged to the U.S. dollar made high-quality Swiss watches a bargain in major markets.

The 1950s and '60s saw Swiss watch brands riding a wave of success, pioneering automatic watches, sporty chronographs, and eventually, the automatic chronograph. By the late 1960s, they had clinched half of the global market, leaving American and Japanese brands struggling to compete.

Then in 1969, Seiko launched the first quartz watch. The Swiss responded in 1970, but these early quartz models were pricey analogs that failed to catch on. Another game-changer came from the U.S., with semiconductor companies improving the technology, leading to LED, then LCD watches—more energy-efficient and always displaying the time.

Meanwhile, the U.S. economy was undergoing its own transformations. Vietnam War expenses and Great Society social programs required the printing of more money. In 1971, President Richard Nixon pulled the plug on dollar-gold convertibility, causing major currencies, including the Swiss Franc, to float freely. The Franc soared, sending Swiss watch prices sky-high.

By 1977, the Japanese had risen to the top. The country's centralized watch industry had quickly pivoted to quartz production, and their quartz watches undercut Swiss prices thanks to cost-effective manufacturing. The Swiss, with their more fragmented industry, struggled to keep up as cheaper Japanese watches inundated the market. Between 1970 and the early '80s, Switzerland's watch landscape was decimated—1,000 of its 1,600 brands vanished, and job losses were massive. Survival demanded a radical rethink, a challenge Breitling was about to face head-on.

Wir unterst
Uhrenarbeiter in
um Arbeit
Gewerkschafts
DES PLACES DE
TRAVAIL – ELLE
DEMANDE PAS
LA LUNE
NOS EMPLOIS
AINTIEN DES POSTES DE TRAVAIL
OUR
OUS

# 1979

# 1994

1979 - 1994
# A NEW BEGINNING

The 1970s was the decade of the Concorde and disco balls, but the quartz crisis made it a dark time for Swiss watchmaking. The cold winds of technological change and global economic pressures had swept away Switzerland's dominance. Inexpensive quartz watches, combined with Willy Breitling's ill health, had come to a head and his sons, Gregory and Alain, were too young to take over the family business. Breitling needed a new owner or its 95 years of watchmaking would end. They say, "Cometh the hour, cometh the man," but to the uninitiated, Ernest Schneider must have seemed a strange choice when he was approached to take on the mantle. On the plus side, he was an electronics engineer and a pilot with a love of aviation. And as the owner of the Sicura watch brand, a specialist in quartz, he was weathering the crisis, even if only just. But to sell the company's heritage to an outsider was a leap in the dark after three generations of Breitling family innovation. Despite any misgivings, the deal was done, and the rest, as they say, is history. After a hesitant start, Ernest launched the new Chronomat and brought the company back to life. To everyone's relief, Breitling's future was secure once more.

# 75

## CHANGING HANDS: WILLY BREITLING TO ERNEST SCHNEIDER

If the 1960s saw Breitling riding the crest of popular culture, with its watches on the wrists of movers and shakers, the following decade was a different story. Cheap quartz watches turned off Switzerland's exports like a tap, and its famed watchmakers were laid off in droves. By 1979, as Willy Breitling's health further deteriorated, his famous factory was shut.

Step forward Georges Caspari, who had been Willy's advertising lynchpin since the 1950s, and had overseen the spectacular marketing successes of the Navitimer, Top Time, and SuperOcean.

Caspari thought a competitor, Ernest Schneider, had a winning strategy. His Sicura brand had survived the crisis by using Swiss-made quartz movements in lower-cost watches.

Ernest's family remembers his stunned silence when Caspari's phone call was put through, followed by "an enthusiastic profanity." He signed a deal to buy the Breitling brand soon after. For the first few years, the company's new beginning seemed to falter, but within three years a new team was in place, the precursor to the Chronomat was on the drawing board, and Breitling was back in the game.

# 76

## THE POWER OF TECHNOLOGY

Ernest Schneider's electronics engineering background gave him vital skills to succeed in the new age of digital watchmaking. Where Willy Breitling's LED and LCD Navitimers had been an unsuccessful roll of the dice, Ernest's quartz models were a new beginning.

His 1980 Breitling catalog contained a blizzard of electronic watches that set the tone for greater things to come. He was never afraid to experiment, so while the Navitimer-branded Mars, Jupiter, and Pluton models showed the way, less attractive innovations like the quartz Top Time quietly vanished without a trace.

Breitling's mastery of microelectronics reached a peak in the life-saving Emergency of 1995, and went further still six years later with the launch of the COSC-certified SuperQuartz movement. Its thermo-compensation altered the timekeeping depending on the temperature of the oscillating crystal, making it 10 times more accurate than its predecessor.

Breitling's success after the dark days of the late 1970s was driven by experimentation and skill, in a balance of traditional watchmaking and new technology that continues to this day.

*BELOW*
*Ad for Breitling's quartz Navitimers*

1979
1994

# 77

# 1980
# PLUTON 80190
## THE ORIGINAL PROFESSIONAL

These were difficult years. Between buying Breitling in 1979 and the breakthrough of his Frecce Tricolori in 1983, Ernest Schneider was casting around for a future direction. Under pressure, he quickly launched a series of quartz models. The Pluton had a screw-in caseback and a Swiss movement with two time zones, a stopwatch, and date. A Navitimer in name more than spirit, it nevertheless helped to define a new Professional range.

# 78

## HARRISON FORD: FLYING SOLO

The *Star Wars* and *Indiana Jones* star was caught on film circa 1984 enjoying a quiet tea time while sporting a rare Navitimer Pluton 2100 PVD. The watch was a special design assigned to the French air force. And while the captain of the *Millennium Falcon* would not become a real-life pilot for another decade, his choice of timepiece was a sign of things to come.

1979
1994

# 79

# RIDERS ON THE STORM: FRECCE TRICOLORI AND AN END TO THE QUARTZ CRISIS

*RIGHT*
*Italy's Frecce Tricolori jet display team*

Designing a chronograph for Italy's Frecce Tricolori jet display team was a turning point in Breitling's fortunes. Three years after taking over, Ernest Schneider had a plan, and people around him who were up to the challenge. Much as Willy Breitling had consulted the Aircraft Owners and Pilots Association to develop the Navitimer 30 years earlier, Ernest worked with the team's pilots to develop a watch that met their needs in and out of the cockpit.

His 1982 sketch of rider tabs, produced when the overall design was well underway, gives an insight into his thinking. The project was entitled "Robust Chrono-Automatic," and the drawing shows "screwed riders" for a rotating bezel. A further comment calls for a study on a curved crystal. They were innovations that came from his own experience as a pilot and from his observations of the display team in action. He later said he'd watched pilots knocking their watches against the metal framework as they opened their canopies on landing.

By slightly recessing a curved glass beneath protective raised rider tabs, he cut down on the number of pilots who returned to base with smashed crystals—and at the same time created a feature that would make Breitling watches distinctive for years to come.

The Frecce Tricolori was an instant success. When it was released for sale in 1984, the Chrono-Automatic project name was shortened to Chronomat, an abbreviation that matched Willy Breitling's contraction of "Chronograph for Mathematicians" for the original slide-rule Chronomat, almost 50 years earlier.

Raised to help protect the glass and aid rotation of the bezel while wearing gloves, the rider tabs were held in place by a screw. The 15 and 45 markers could be swapped to enable the reading of remaining or elapsed time, a Breitling signature that persists.

It was an inspired decision to use a simplified automatic chronograph movement that hadn't been made since the quartz crisis. The first movements were assembled from stockpiles of unused parts, but the Chronomat's success helped to restart production of a movement that's so reliable, Breitling has used it ever since.

Viewed from the side, the case bears a resemblance to a jet aircraft in a tribute to the pilots who wore it. At 15 mm thick and around 39 mm across, its size was a deliberate statement of intent, over and above the proportions needed to accommodate the automatic movement and provide 100 meters of water resistance.

19
79

# 80

19
94

# 1983
# FRECCE TRICOLORI
## RETURN OF THE MECHANICAL CHRONOGRAPH

To the newly identified Yuppies watching *Tron* on their VCRs, the future was digital. But Ernest Schneider tapped into a desire for the traditional and the mechanical. Consultation with Italy's jet display team, the Frecce Tricolori, resulted in a perfectly engineered instrument for pilots with innovations set to last; raised rider tabs on a rotating bezel, and the glass slightly recessed to protect it from damage. The distinctive Rouleaux bracelet sets off a chronograph that will change the company's fortunes as the Chronomat.

19
79

19
94

# 8

## CHRONOMAT
## DESIGN EVOLUTION

**1984**
### CHRONOMAT 81950

Breitling's centenary release flies in the face of the quartz revolution. The sturdy Frecce Tricolori, with its Valjoux 7750 movement, gets the Chronomat name and the new wings-and-anchor logo. A giant among all-purpose sports watches is born.

**2001**
### CHRONOMAT

Now a "grand totalizer," it's even available with diamonds that sparkle around bold tool-watch subdials (because why not?). Check the time and you see wings and two anchors. This is a chronograph for every eventuality.

**2005**
### CHRONOMAT EVOLUTION

Breitling's jet display team is making headlines and the Chronomat has evolved in the slipstream of the fast, the noisy, and the spectacular. The eighties' original was no shrinking violet in its day and neither is this big new interpretation.

**2009**
### CHRONOMAT B01 44

The launch model for Breitling's much-anticipated exclusive chronograph movement, the Manufacture Caliber 01. Five years in development, it crowns 125 years of watchmaking heritage. The smoothed-down bezel will become standard.

2014
### CHRONOMAT 44 RAVEN

Owner Theodore Schneider's forthright style is wrapped up in 44 mm of carbon-based coating and uncompromising orange. Breitling makes watches for "rugged individualists," he explains, "driving the fastest cars… feeling strong and free."

2020
### CHRONOMAT B01 42

Redesigned, refined, every inch a modern chronograph. CEO Georges Kern slims down the proportions, flattens the rider tabs, and reinvents the classic Rouleaux bracelet. The "script B" logo returns for a Chronomat with new mission.

2021
### SUPER CHRONOMAT

The boldest Chronomat yet, with ceramic updates to its classic Frecce Tricolori features. There's a four-year calendar version and a new Rouleaux-inspired rubber strap. The classic UTC module is perfect for the frequent flyer.

2022
### CHRONOMAT GMT 40

At 40 millimeters, and with a standout red second-time-zone hand, it's the everyday interpretation of the legendary design. Water-resistant to 200 meters and with a clean all-steel design, it has wearability and style in spades.

19
79

19
94

# 82

## SUPER CHRONOMAT B19
## 140TH ANNIVERSARY

In another creative first, Breitling has introduced a skeletonized watch with a movement redesigned and re-engineered to allow you to see through multiple layers of its components. The perpetual calendar of the Super Chronomat B19 44 Perpetual Calendar 140th Anniversary updates a heritage that stretches back to the legendary chronograph created for the Frecce Tricolori jet display team in 1983. The rubber strap and ceramic inserts underline Breitling's place as the inventor of the modern chronograph.

BREITLING
1884
TACHYMETER
SWISS
MADE
SAT SUN MON TUE WED THU FRI
OCT DEC FEB APR JUN AUG

Mets

# 83

## JERRY SEINFELD: PRIME TIME

In his eponymous 1990s sitcom *Seinfeld*, the comedian was rarely seen without a Chronomat. The one time he notably doffed his Breitling timepiece? When his onscreen parents gave him a substandard watch as a gift. And while that watch would end up in a New York City trash can (with much ensuing high jinks), the show famously "about nothing" would go on ticking for a remarkable 180 episodes.

*RIGHT*
*The Breitling Jet Team*

# 84

## 100% AERONAUTICS: A NEW FOCUS FOR A NEW ERA

The Schneiders' journey to a promotional strategy that became known as "100% Aeronautics" developed over the first few years of their ownership. Ernest Schneider was a pilot, and he was advised by Breitling's long-time advertising mastermind, Georges Caspari, whose success at marketing the Navitimer in the 1950s convinced Ernest of the value of tapping into the prestige that aviation offered.

A slew of new logos on his first Breitling models showed how his thinking developed. First came the familiar "script B" with an anchor, and for his quartz Navitimers—and the first automatic Chronomats—there were wings and a wave. It didn't take him long to combine both ideas, with a more stylish pair of wings joining the anchor and a straightened B. From then on, flight was an indelible part of the brand.

At a time when collaborations were being recognized as a path to commercial success, Ernest put his wings logo on the dial of his 1984 Chronomat to complement the advertising deal he'd agreed to with the Frecce Tricolori aerobatics team. The prestige of fast jets contributed to the Chronomat's popularity and proved the potential of aviation partnerships. Sponsorship of aerobatic competitions followed soon after, leading to the Breitling World Cup of Aerobatics, which saw aircraft flying the brand's colors across the globe.

The Breitling Aviation Academy was founded in 1994, significantly scaling up the strategy. It prepared established aerobatics pilots for top-level competition and trained talented up-and-comers.

By the turn of the millennium, an aviation manager, Stefano Albinati, had been appointed, and with Ernest's son Theodore in charge, the strategy was turbocharged.

Their first joint coup was the Breitling Orbiter's nonstop round-the-world balloon flight in 1999, the same year that a squad of historic World War II aircraft—the Breitling Fighters—began performing at airshows. Aerobatics sponsorship produced the Breitling Jet Team, then the Breitling Wingwalkers, with female acrobats performing ballet in the sky. Theodore's last big aviation adventure was to support the restoration of the Douglas DC-3 that went on an epic journey around the world in 2017.

Many of the partnerships were tied to model launches or promotions; from the Chronomat to the Fighters Navitimer and the revolutionary Emergency. The Schneiders' 100% Aeronautics strategy gave them what they liked to call "wings of success" for nearly four decades.

BREITLING
AMERICAN TOUR
ES-YLI
BREITLING Jet Team

*TOP*
***The Breitling Jet Team***

*ABOVE*
***The Breitling Wingwalkers***

*RIGHT*
***The Breitling Angels***

SPIN
BREITLING
Angels
BREITLING

19
79

19
94

# 85

1985

# AEROSPACE 80360

## QUARTZ MASTERPIECE

Imagine yourself in charge of Breitling in 1985. Last year's Chronomat was a huge success, heralding the return of the mechanical, but quartz still dominated. What now? Ernest Schneider's next move was the Aerospace 80360. It combined his experience in quartz with a forensic eye for detail. Titanium, 9 mm thick, with an analog-digital display, it became a pilots' favorite. Forgive its short-lived appropriation of the Navitimer name and acknowledge a watch that defined flying for decades.

19
79

19
94

# 86

***"I never found exactly what I wanted right off the bat; it was always Breitling that explained what it wanted."***

*ERNEST SCHNEIDER*

19
79

# 87

19
94

1985

# OLD NAVITIMER 81600

## MECHANICAL ONCE MORE

Mark Twain famously described a report of his death as an exaggeration. A Lemania movement in a rereleased Navitimer showed that tears shed for mechanical timepieces had been equally premature. "Someday all watches will be made this way" went the slogan for the first quartz models. But Breitling's new owner, Ernest Schneider, disagreed. Someday, he thought, a 1980s revival of the hand-wound Navitimer would be a valuable collector's item. Time would prove him right.

# 88

## SERGE GAINSBOURG: WRIST REBELLION

In the days before official brand ambassadors, singer and artist Serge Gainsbourg captured attention on and off the stage in his Breitling Navitimer 81600. It was the end of the quartz crisis, and Gainsbourg's chosen watch was the first Navitimer of the mechanical revival. Always the provocateur, Gainsbourg even commissioned a special rally-style bracelet in platinum.

GITANES

19
94

20
17

# 1994 - 2017
# STATE OF THE ART

Succession, the handing over of an enterprise from one generation to the next, can be uplifting, like *The Lion King*, or dramatic, like the hit TV drama of the same name that spanned four seasons. With two willful characters like Ernest and Theodore Schneider, the handover was a mix of the two. Individually and together, father and son proved a formidable force. Theodore moved Breitling with the times, producing iconic watches that chimed with an era of opulence, giving Ernest the breathing space to continue Breitling's heritage of pushing boundaries with his revolutionary Emergency watch. Theodore—Thedy to his friends—was an accomplished pilot who was enthralled by aviation in all its forms. He combined passions for watches and military aircraft with uncompromising leadership as he came in and out of Breitling in the 1980s. He took official control in 1994, and went on to create a considerable legacy: from unforgettable aviation-themed marketing to the creation of Breitling's first in-house movement and the construction of the state-of-the-art Breitling Chronometrie in La Chaux-de-Fonds.

# 89

## CHANGING HANDS: ERNEST SCHNEIDER TO THEODORE SCHNEIDER

The Breitling handover from Ernest Schneider to his son, Theodore, was a transfer from aviation enthusiast to aviation fanatic. They were both pilots and had worked side by side at Breitling in the early 1980s until Theodore left, citing "incompatibility of temperament." He eventually returned in 1989 and took over full-time in 1994.

Theodore appreciated Breitling's back catalog, cherishing the Navitimer and reintroducing complications like the rattrapante, but he did things his own way. He fostered a tight management structure and wasn't afraid to wield a duster in the lead-up to a new boutique opening.

His love of fast, noisy planes was harnessed to market the big, macho watches that defined Breitling for a generation. They were created, read a mission statement at one memorable watch fair, "for all the rugged individualists who dream of flying a fighter jet, but will settle for driving the fastest cars, seducing the most beautiful women, feeling unique, strong, and free. And that's a lot of people."

Theodore summed up Breitling's strategy under his leadership in three sentences: "We believed in never looking back. Never holding back. And never apologizing."

*ABOVE*
*For COSC testing, movements are provided with plain white dials and basic black hands*

# 90

## COSC CERTIFICATION: TESTED TO PERFECTION

For the uninitiated, a *chronograph* is a timepiece with stopwatch functions, while a *chronometer* is a watch that has been tested to exacting standards.

From the mid-1980s until 1999, those in the know could identify a Breitling chronometer by the "3" in the center of its model number. A Chronomat A13050 chronograph was not a chronometer, while the A13350 was both. It was little understood by customers, who might have assumed that all Breitling watches had passed the most stringent tests.

In 1999 Breitling made the brave decision to have every watch—mechanical and quartz—certified as a chronometer to earn its billing as an instrument for professionals.

The Swiss Official Chronometer Testing Institute, COSC, was chosen as the ultimate authority for certification. In one stroke Breitling added its entire output to the tiny percentage of Swiss watches—less than one in 30—that previously had been awarded the coveted status.

The decision would lead to the construction of the new Breitling Chronometrie two years later, and then to the development of in-house movements that continue to open up opportunities for even more precision and ever-improving quality control.

19
94

20
17

# 91
## BREITLING ORBITER
## A BALLOON AROUND THE WORLD

Of all the epic aviation displays, sponsorships, and tie-ins that Theodore Schneider put the brand's weight behind, none had the global impact of the Breitling Orbiter 3 in 1999. The first nonstop around-the-world balloon flight was an adventure that attracted global media attention and put Breitling on the cover of *National Geographic* magazine. The balloon, and the Breitling name, appeared on postage stamps in Switzerland and Monaco. Theodore was delighted: "Until the evening before Orbiter 3 set off, people sometimes had to be told how to write Breitling. After this adventure, there was no longer any need to spell out the name."

The idea began as a simple sponsorship of Bertrand Piccard to promote the Breitling Aerospace in the transatlantic balloon race. He won it with the watch on, and a longtime partnership was born.

Piccard dreamed of achieving the century's major aeronautical challenge: to circumnavigate the globe nonstop in a balloon carried by jet streams 7,000 to 12,000 meters above sea level. Supported by Breitling, he set off in 1997 in Orbiter 1 but had to ditch in the Mediterranean with technical problems. Theodore arranged for his rescue and pledged to continue his support. The following year Piccard tried again, only to be defeated by international airspace restrictions, but not before setting the record for the longest balloon-flight duration.

By then, 18 separate teams had announced plans to take the record and seven of them had launched a total of 16 balloons in unsuccessful attempts.

Theodore was determined to succeed and took a hands-on role as the sole sponsor for the final attempt. Stefano Albinati, Breitling's resourceful head of aeronautics, set up a group of experts to improve the mission's chances. He oversaw improvements to the structure of the 55-meter Rozier-style balloon, which combined helium and hot-air technologies. An impressive ground team was assembled, with leading meteorologists to direct the balloon toward the most favorable jet streams, and air traffic controllers with the clout to negotiate flight clearances around the globe.

On March 1, 1999, Breitling Orbiter 3 ascended from Châteaux-d'Oex, in the Swiss Alps, carrying Bertrand Piccard and Brian Jones, each equipped with an Emergency watch with a built-in distress beacon transmitter. Global media coverage followed their epic journey and they landed 19 days, 21 hours, and 47 minutes later in the Egyptian desert, having traveled 45,633 km (28,355 miles). In celebration, Theodore produced a 250-piece limited edition of the Emergency with the Orbiter logo on the dial.

The Breitling Orbiter 3 capsule has been on display in the Smithsonian National Air and Space Museum in Washington, D.C., USA, ever since. Its journey was a true world event, summed up by Queen Elizabeth, who spoke for adventure enthusiasts all over the world when she said: "The news of your splendid achievement has delighted us all."

BREITLING
ORBITER 3

BREITLING
BREITLING

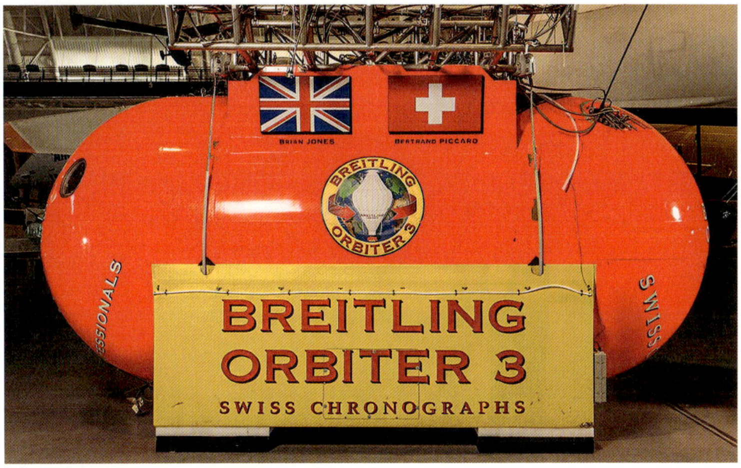


LEFT
*Balloon pilots Bertrand Piccard and Brian Jones*

TOP
*Orbiter 3 touches down in Egypt after its round-the-world voyage*

ABOVE
*The unmistakable capsule is on display at the Smithsonian*

# 92

## GRENCHEN HQ: TWENTY-FIRST-CENTURY ARCHITECTURE

The municipality of Grenchen, Switzerland, has a long history of watchmaking, and it was Ernest Schneider's base when he became Breitling's owner. By the turn of the millennium, the company needed more space and better facilities. Construction of an assembly, quality control, and customer service center in 2000 was the start of a series of stylish new buildings for Breitling's operations, all designed by the Swiss architect Alain Porta.

To complement Grenchen's award-winning architectural heritage, Porta echoed the natural-light admitting features of traditional watchmaking workshops with large strips of glazing. The walls are clad in Italian *pietra dorata*, a stone that became a signature of all the Breitling buildings that followed. "Amid these rather 'hard' architectures, it serves to enliven the facades by bringing a more vibrant element," Porta explained.

The headquarters itself was restructured in the same architectural style. To highlight Breitling's links with aviation, it featured photography signed by the aerial star photographer Katsuhiko Tokunaga, who had long been a collaborative partner, as well as a panoramic terrace with a life-size reproduction of the legendary Spitfire aircraft.

# 93 KEVIN T. KELLY: BREITLING AND THE NEW POP ART

"I was selling my pop art through the Bruce R. Lewin gallery in SoHo, New York. One day, around 1999, Bruce calls me up and says, 'Hey, a collector likes your work and wants to commission some pieces. He's into World War II fighter aircraft and expensive Swiss watches.' And the first thing I thought was, 'I'm not painting any watches.'

The 'collector' turned out to be Theodore Schneider. At the time I was doing a series about relationships, so I came up with the idea of a man and a woman, in a relationship of some sort, arguing and kissing, embracing, right up to... you know, NSFW stuff. And then in the background these fighter aircraft would be a metaphor for what was going on.

I sent him 10 sketches and he ended up commissioning eight of them for the Breitling Headquarters. They had a sort of dark humor that I think he responded to. Ten years later, they were used around the world in the Breitling boutiques.

Nowadays, I paint landscapes, but I still sell those prints to people who remember them as a great part of Breitling's history."

**KEVIN T. KELLY**

*The American artist, whose work still hangs in Breitling headquarters, is known for his neo-pop art, described as "Roy Lichtenstein meets Dennis Hopper on steroids."*

# 94

# THE BREITLING CHRONOMETRIE LA CHAUX-DE-FONDS

Long before Leon Breitling was born, wealthy Europeans were flocking to Switzerland for its healthy climate. In the words of English novelist Mary Shelley: "The fresh air and bright sun seldom failed to restore me."

But the famed Swiss climate was found to be lacking when a decision was taken to build a new Breitling watchmaking center of excellence in La Chaux-de-Fonds, the original home of Leon's business. The air, 1,000 meters above sea level in the Jura mountains, was still not good enough for one of the most technically advanced watch factories Switzerland had ever seen.

The Breitling Chronometrie, designed by Swiss architect Alain Porta as an elegant addition to the city's UNESCO World Heritage status, opened in 2001. It would ensure that Breitling could deliver on its commitment to have every movement certified by the Swiss Official Chronometer Testing Institute (COSC). With increasing demand for Breitling watches, an ultra-modern design and assembly facility was essential.

It took just eight months to build, repeating design elements from the new headquarters recently opened in Grenchen, including a broad, nearly 80-meter-long glazed strip running along the entire facade.

The new Chronometrie was designed to eliminate two of the principal enemies of a watch movement: moisture and dust. The mountain air had to be improved, the dust filtered out, and the humidity precisely controlled. Using positive air pressure in the most sensitive areas, a new generation of ultra-precise watch movements could be consistently produced to perform accurately for years to come.

In rooms ventilated like medical facilities, with the air completely renewed every 10 minutes, Breitling movements start their long journey from individual parts to completed chronometer. The most critical components are checked one by one to tolerances as fine as one thousandth of a millimeter. Automation takes over for assembly processes where the skills of even the most experienced watchmaker can be bettered; crucial lubrication is administered in precise amounts by robots.

Eight years after opening, with sales increasing and an urgent need to develop an in-house caliber, the Chronometrie's footprint was tripled to accommodate the high-tech manufacture and assembly of the Breitling Manufacture Caliber 01 movement and its derivatives that continue to break new ground today. Once again, automation complements human expertise; the 346 individual components of Caliber 01 are automatically combined into 76 elements and 41 screws before highly skilled watchmakers assemble them by hand.

Across the entire range, the heart of the process is the chronometry workshop where accuracy is adjusted to tenths, hundredths, and even thousandths of a second. In the hands of experts, a tiny hole is bored by hand to align the balance wheel, a critical operation that relies on many years of experience. One wrong move, and the movement could be rejected. Only now, with everything tested, and tested again, can the completed caliber be submitted to the COSC laboratories for certification as an official chronometer.

By the time a Breitling chronometer leaves the Breitling Chronometrie it will have accumulated around a thousand checks, over 10 laborious months, in a watchmaking facility like no other.

19
94

20
17

# 95

2000

# CHRONO AVENGER

## INDUSTRIAL INFLUENCE

Dance floors will soon reverberate to Daft Punk's "Harder, Better, Faster, Stronger," its robotic lyric declaring work is never over, and Breitling launches a chronograph to match the era's cyber energy. An oversize crown and hefty screw-down pushers are set in a block of solid titanium. "Raw power" is the tagline and space-age military is the look. Welcome to the new millennium with the latest aviation range, billed as "The essence of Breitling."

19
94

20
17

# 96

# AVENGER DESIGN EVOLUTION

2002
### AVENGER SEAWOLF

The resilient Avenger case is further adapted to withstand a 3,000 meter dive, with input from the Swiss Federal Institute of Technology. The pressure-relief valve and high-grip crown are backed up with a crystal almost 5 mm thick.

2003
### SUPER AVENGER CHRONOGRAPH 48

Would you dare to wear a 48.4 mm steel chronograph 18 mm thick? It's a challenge that pays off when the watch advertised as reflecting Breitling's "full force and personality" becomes one of the most popular models.

2019
### AVENGER AUTOMATIC 43

You want compact, elegant, and still action-fueled? This is it. Water-resistant to 300 meters, sharp, and highly legible. You can operate the bezel while wearing gloves, but it's as much at home in the boardroom as the cockpit.

2021
### AVENGER AUTOMATIC GMT 45 NIGHT MISSION

A shock-resistant tool watch whose titanium case is cloaked in diamond-hard black carbon. The yellow GMT hand makes the second time zone instantly legible. It's a rugged combo of military and go-anywhere style.

2022
### AVENGER B01 CHRONOGRAPH 45

The top-selling Avenger gains Breitling's Manufacture Caliber 01 and ups its impact on the wrist. Red accents stand out on the dial and sweep hand, and the polished rider tabs highlight the satin finish.

2023
### AVENGER B01 CHRONOGRAPH 44

The big performance aviation watch gets a modern makeover. Square pushers balance the high-grip crown. The distinctive bezel sets off military-colored dials, while the integrated date window adds to the elegance.

2023
### AVENGER B01 CHRONO 44 NIGHT MISSION

A tough cousin of the chrono, in full ceramic with titanium hardware. Its nod to aircraft design materials includes a carbon-fiber dial on the all-black version. Oversized lumed numerals give extra night viz.

# 97

## JOHN TRAVOLTA: A PILOT'S SENSIBILITY

The film director Quentin Tarantino described John Travolta as one of the greatest movie stars Hollywood has ever produced. But it was his aviation history that clinched his signing as a Breitling ambassador in 2005. He was famously an experienced pilot and plane enthusiast who'd used his first acting paychecks to cover flying lessons, racking up more than 9,000 current flight hours and, to Theodore Schneider's delight, a collection of aircraft in his own backyard. Breitling ads featuring the star appeared with the strap lines "Profession: Pilot. Career. Actor" and "Welcome to Our World."

# 98

## BREITLING MANUFACTURE CALIBER 01: THE FIRST IN-HOUSE MOVEMENT

*RIGHT*
*An exploded view of Breitling's Manufacture Caliber 01*

At the start of the new millennium, with the crisis years of the 1970s a fading memory, the future for Breitling seemed to be assured. But rumbling in the background was a potential problem.

Leon, Gaston, and Willy Breitling had sourced accurate and reliable movements that they could enhance in-house. Ernest Schneider had adopted the same approach, turning blank Valjoux 7750 parts into the COSC-certified caliber B13. As a business model it was eventually thwarted by the march of globalization, and the mergers and acquisitions that came in its wake. By 2002 the Swiss watch industry was buying three quarters of its movements from one manufacturer, which suddenly announced it would restrict supplies as of 2006.

The Swiss Competition Commission stepped in and pushed the cut-off date to 2010, while Breitling pondered whether there was time to gather the expertise and create the infrastructure to produce an all-new chronograph movement in-house.

The momentous decision to go ahead was made in 2004, and the idea was developed in the utmost secrecy under the acronym PFI; because the new movement would power the "professional flight instruments" of the future. The aim was to create a technical, modern, and reliable caliber that could serve as a foundation for Breitling watches for generations to come. It would have to be a self-winding chronograph that could consistently pass the COSC tests and provide flexibility for future model development.

Within a few months the movement's overall architecture was established, and the main technical options agreed upon. The first parts were assembled in the spring of 2006, and remarkably, just a year later, the Breitling Manufacture Caliber 01 was produced in its final form.

A column-wheel system was combined with a vertical clutch that could ensure perfectly clean starts of the chronograph function with no risk of making the hand jump, and no chance of discrepancies among the various displays. The power reserve was more than 70 hours, allowing it to keep time off the wrist for up to three days, and improving the timekeeping. To make it even easier to use, an instant date change allowed corrections at any time, with no danger of damaging the mechanism.

Plans were produced to extend the Breitling Chronometrie in La Chaux-de-Fonds, and by early 2009, Breitling Chronometrie 2 was beginning the meticulous task of creating the new caliber at scale for its official introduction.

The heart of the process to this day sums up the ethos of the entire achievement—a mingling of the traditional and the high-tech. The assembly line is a runway on which humans and machines work together in a continuous, highly choreographed dance. When each Caliber 01 comes off the line, it is ready to be sent off to the COSC for the ultimate test of reliability and accuracy, and true to the original design requirements, few need to go back for adjustment.

The Caliber 01 was the beginning of a new chapter in Breitling's history, the Breitling spirit, engineered perfectly.

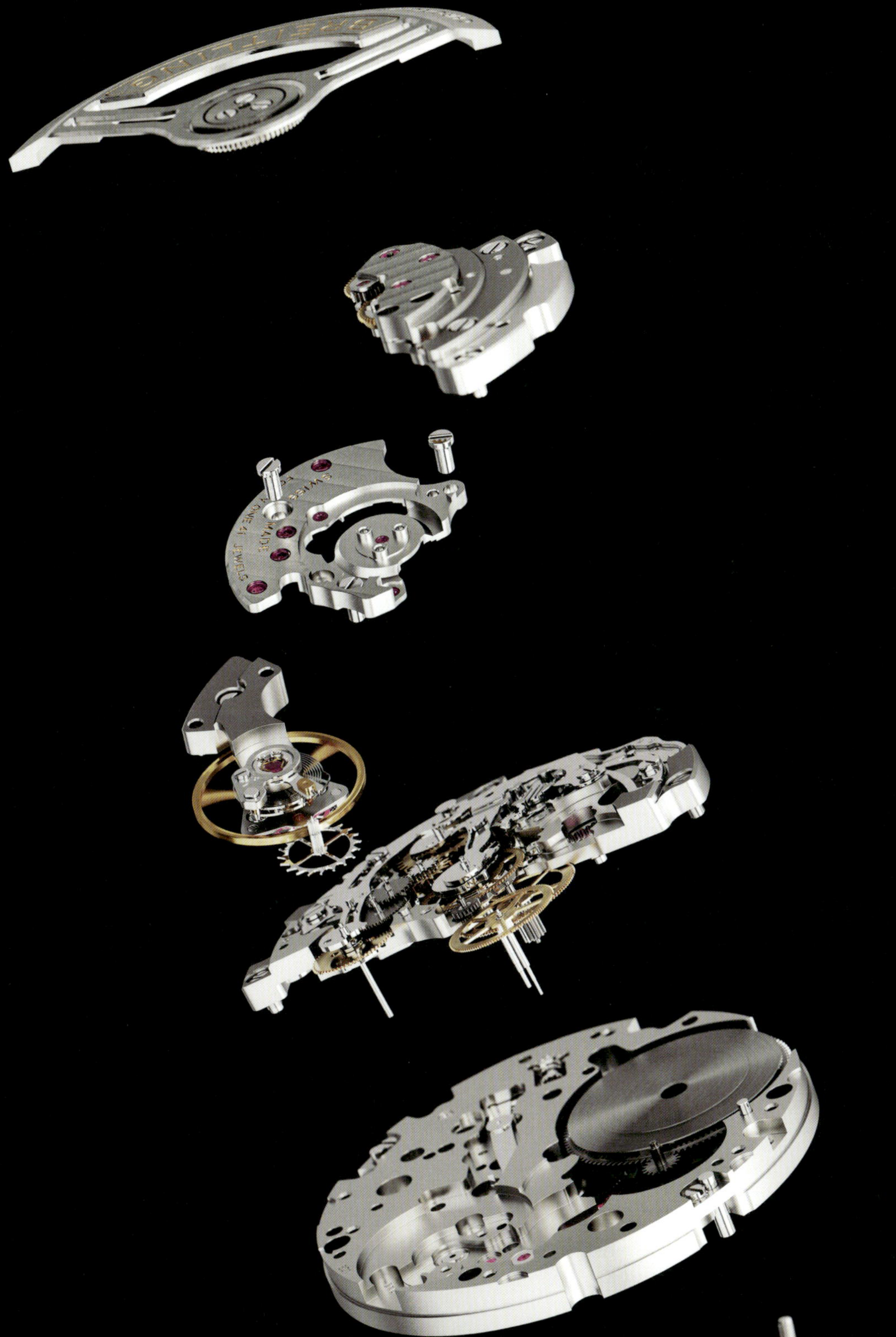

# 99

## INSTRUMENTS FOR PROFESSIONALS

Aircraft and watches were the Schneiders' passions, and they spent freely on one to promote the other. Sponsoring wingwalkers and bankrolling jet display teams could serve two purposes—the daredevil stunts gave the Schneiders their aviation kick while attracting customers who wanted the performance of a pilot's chronograph. They needed a marketing slogan that would do justice to their strategy.

In 1990 they found it. The professionalism of pilots who relied on Breitling's advanced timing instruments had always been something that customers could aspire to. "Instruments for Professionals" was born, a catchphrase that would have chimed with Leon Breitling's business in the 1880s.

It appeared on ads for the new Chronomat next to pictures of jets and the assurance: "Our obsession is quality. Our goal is performance." Navitimers and Avengers were "Designed for service in the demanding, split-second world of fighter aircraft."

Crucially, the slogan softened the one criticism that might be leveled against an all-out campaign for aviators. "Instruments for Professionals" broadened the appeal to customers everywhere. "Breitling never confined its ambitions to a niche market," Theodore Schneider wrote, "however prestigious."

# 100

## BREITLING JET TEAM

Pilot Jacques Bothelin established the Apache Aviation aerobatics display team in 1981. By the time he hooked up with fellow aviation enthusiast Theodore Schneider he'd flown more than 8,000 hours in more than 100 different aircraft. Theodore recognized a kindred spirit, and in 2003 they agreed on a sponsorship deal for the world's only civilian jet display team.

The Breitling Jet Team started off flying four Aero L-39C Albatros military training jets, eventually increasing to seven. The professional pilots, many with experience in fighter jets, put on displays flying less than three meters apart at nearly 700 km/h, and performed to standards expected from national display teams.

Life-size statues of the pilots were placed in boutiques, and flights were offered to lucky reporters. In Theodore's words: "Invite a journalist to fly in one of the Breitling Jet Team's planes and they will have grasped the entire Breitling philosophy."

19
94

20
17

*RIGHT*
*Breitling's first-ever boutique opened in New York City, 2010*

# 101

## A NEW YORK DEBUT

If you can make it there, you'll make it anywhere, goes the eponymous song about New York. Breitling was definitely channeling Sinatra's sentiment when it opened its very first brand boutique on New York City's tony 57th Street in 2010, marking a retail milestone. "At the time, watches were sold through multi-brand stores, so a dedicated boutique was unprecedented," noted Thierry Prissert, president of Breitling North America. "We were the first in the city. The first anywhere." The boutique's design, a collaboration with Theodore Schneider's trusted architect Alain Porta, echoed the Swiss headquarters with walnut floors and *pietra dorata* stone, complemented by Kevin T. Kelly's neo-pop art. "Thedy was on top of every detail," said Prissert. "He ran his finger over a surface and found dust. It was December 20, right before the holidays, and he took me down Madison Avenue to find a specific vacuum that he then used himself on the whole boutique. He said, 'You see that? That's how I want it done.'" A Miami location quickly followed, and today Breitling's worldwide store count is in the hundreds. Meanwhile, the original NYC boutique (one of three in the city) has since relocated to a spectacular all-glass storefront on the corner of Madison and 57th. "It's unbelievable to look back and say we started that movement," Prissert reflected.

*ABOVE*
*Astronauts Sergey Volkov (left) and Scott Kelly repair a Chronomat on the ISS*

# 102

## ORBITAL WATCHWORKS

In December 2015, while orbiting Earth on the International Space Station, astronaut Scott Kelly ran into an unexpected mission: repairing crewmate Sergey Volkov's Chronomat bracelet.

A quick satellite call to Kelly's astronaut twin brother on Earth, and a Breitling repair kit was en route to space as part of a shipment of ISS supplies. The result? A successful zero-G timepiece fix and a record-book moment for Breitling.

BREITLING
3

# 103

## THE BREITLING WINGWALKERS

The AeroSuperBatics—aka Breitling Wingwalkers—in their flight over Bahrain were captured by the legendary Japanese air-to-air photographer Katsuhiko Tokunaga. Pilot Dave Barrell, who flew one of the Breitling-emblazoned Boeing Stearmans with an acrobat on his wing, says he had the time of his life during the sponsorship that ran from 2010 to 2017: "We had dinner with John Travolta and Katy Perry. It was a great seven years!"

# 104

## EMERGENCY: A WATCH THAT SAVES LIVES

The history of ideas, of human nature's relentless drive to go further and do better, is a timeline of great individuals, chance, and opportunity. Breitling's creation of the world's first watch with a built-in dual-frequency distress beacon involved all three.

The idea for the Emergency came to Ernest Schneider after a conversation with a NATO officer. Ernest had proved with his new Aerospace chronograph that electronics could provide the reliability that pilots needed, while military officials wanted to improve the chances of rescuing personnel in the event of an emergency. Might it be possible, the two men wondered, to miniaturize a distress transmitter so that pilots could always carry one with them, like a watch? Ernest, with his training in electronics engineering and almost two decades of experience producing quartz watches, had a new goal.

The opportunity for development came from Theodore Schneider's return to Breitling in 1989. As Ernest gradually handed over control of the company, he had more time to devote to a project that would take longer to come to fruition than any other watch in Breitling's long history.

The technical challenges were immense, while waivers and approvals were required from regulators who had never imagined that the technology would be on sale in a watch.

In 1988, marketing material drawn up for a prototype Emergency described it as "A watch that can save lives." Effectively an Aerospace clamped on top of a tiny transmitter in a clamshell case screwed together at one side, it was never mass produced and only two examples are known to have survived.

In official filings in the U.S., the Emergency was a "backup survival instrument intended for use in the event of an aviation accident," but from the outset it was to be marketed to all explorers of air, land, and sea. In 1995, with Theodore running the company full time, Ernest was able to launch his revolutionary watch. Based on the 121.5 MHz international frequency, its novelty continued to put demands on Breitling's technical and legal departments. It took nine months in 1998 to get U.K. aircraft equipment approval for the Emergency Locator Watch. U.S. authorizations took even longer. But the Emergency was a resounding success, with almost 40,000 sold by 2009.

In 2013, the Emergency II updated the offering to make it the first wristwatch with an integrated Personal Locator Beacon using the Cospas-Sarsat international satellite warning system. Capable of digital and analog transmission, it was, and remains, a one-of-a-kind system for locating victims.

Theodore could not resist the aviation opportunities that his new watch presented. Movie-style ads were shot in dramatic locations from California, Texas, and Utah, to Greenland, the French Alps, and the Mediterranean Sea. In one, a Navy rescue helicopter took off from a frigate, another featured a French Civil Security helicopter in the Alps with their chief mountain rescue pilot at the controls.

After more than three decades, the Emergency is a testament to Ernest Schneider's vision and determination. His groundbreaking idea is still on sale, and still saving lives.

BREITLING
1884
EMERGENCY
DIETZ

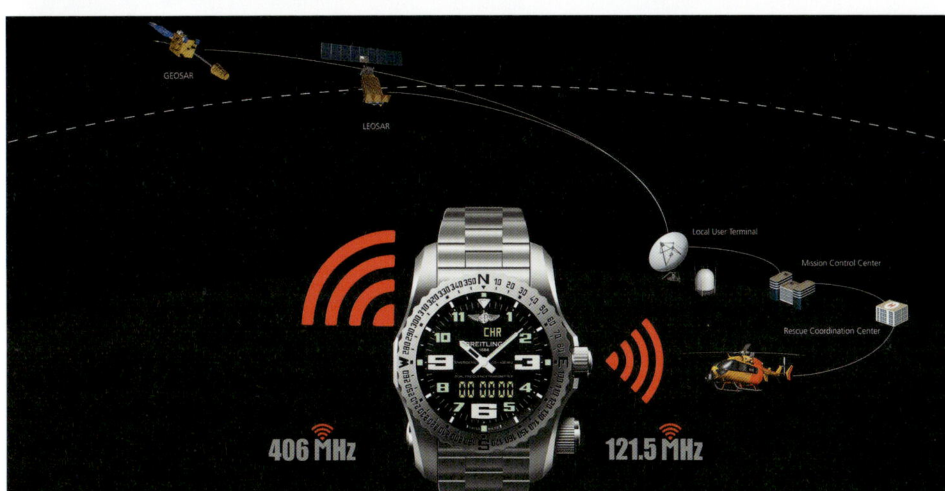


*LEFT*
*An ad for the Emergency focuses on its lifesaving capabilities*

*TOP*
*Schematic showing the placement of the tubular emergency beacon in the watch*

*ABOVE*
*The 121.5 MHz distress frequency has a range of 160 km*

1994
2017

# 105

# 2013
# EMERGENCY II
## LIFESAVING INNOVATION

Ernest Schneider was willing to take risks. The result was a string of groundbreaking watches. His last was a revolutionary model capable of beaming distress signals from anywhere on the planet.
A 1988 prototype for professional use was followed by the commercial release of the Emergency I in 1995. It was the most drawn-out development of any watch in Breitling's history. Its successor is still in production, and still saving lives.

ITLING

*LEFT*
*Richard Branson waves off the Breitling Orbiter I in 1997*



# 106

## RICHARD BRANSON: IN CASE OF EMERGENCY

Entrepreneur, Virgin Group Founder, epic adventurer, and aviation enthusiast Richard Branson held his Breitling Emergency, with its distress beacon transmitter, in the highest regard. "It's saved my life on a couple of occasions," he told a reporter in 2006. The man who tried to beat the Breitling Orbiter in the round-the-world balloon race, said he'd been rescued by helicopter six times. His Emergency has since been acquired for the Breitling collection. "I think the last time I used it was when I was off Tahiti in the Pacific when our balloon went down," he said. "I am very grateful to this watch."

19
94

20
17

# 107 BIG IN JAPAN: CHRONO IN THE LAND OF THE RISING SUN

LEFT
*Kimbara used an educational campaign to introduce Japan to the craftsmanship behind the chronograph*

"In 1991, toward the end of Japan's economic bubble, I embarked on a venture with Osawa Trading, becoming a distributor for Breitling. At that point, the market was inundated with quartz timepieces in gold and diamonds. These watches were like a symbol of the economy itself: their opulence was only on the surface.

We set out to introduce Breitling's mechanical chronographs, such as the Chronomat and the Navitimer, to a clientele largely unfamiliar with what went into a mechanical movement. The perception was that mechanical watches, especially chronographs, were big and complicated.

Faced with a market that was choosing style over substance, we launched an educational campaign. We put out a meticulously designed brochure that revealed the inner mechanics of the chronograph, showing the movement as an intricate universe operating in complete precision. Our goal was to introduce the Japanese consumer to the beauty, sophistication, and history of these pieces.

As the bubble economy burst, there was a pivot toward authenticity and quality. The Japanese, with their deep-seated reverence for fine craftsmanship, began to connect with the artisanal nature of the mechanical chronograph.

We witnessed this cultural shift firsthand through membership in our newly formed Breitling Club, which started modestly but soon swelled. By 1995, Theodore Schneider recognized Osawa's endeavors and proposed a partnership to establish Breitling Japan. Our handshake agreement has since flourished into 16 boutiques and 80 retail outlets across Japan. The Breitling Club, now with 270,000 members, is a testament to the place of reverence the chronograph holds today in Japan."

**ATSUSHI KIMBARA**

*The former president of Breitling Japan worked with the company from 1991 to 2024, spearheading market growth, cultivating appreciation for mechanical watchmaking, and expanding the brand's dedicated following.*

*LEFT*
*A Breitling-branded Douglas DC-3 went on an around-the-world tour in 2017*



# 108

## DC-3 WORLD TOUR

For a man with a love of old planes and a successful history of using them to promote his watch brand, Theodore Schneider's financial support for the restoration and world tour of a World War II Douglas DC-3 was just one more adventure. But this time, he produced a limited edition of iconic watches and took them all with him.

A 1955 Lockheed L-1049 Super Constellation had been the first restoration project in 2004, but the 1940 DC-3 was more of a challenge.

The plane set off in 2017 after more than six months of planning, a feat only possible for a company with its own aviation manager. It visited the Balkans, the Middle East, India, Southeast Asia, China, Japan, the USA, and Europe.

The entire journey was accompanied by 500 Navitimer watches—the DC-3 World Tour limited edition—each with a logbook listing the itinerary, pilots' names, and weather conditions of the 45,374 km (24,500 mile) trip. Their eventual owners could boast their watch had flown around the world in the oldest plane to achieve the feat.

20
17

20
24

## 2017 – 2024

# A MODERN-RETRO BRAND

The way we think about the big things in life tends to shift imperceptibly until we look back and wonder why it took us so long. One such cultural shift was captured by a new word and a viral hashtag in the same year that Georges Kern became Breitling's CEO. The 2017 *Oxford Dictionary*'s word of the year was *Youthquake*—"change arising from the actions of young people." "Society is changing," Georges said in one of his first interviews as CEO, "Breitling can have influence with our activities, our celebrities, and our campaigns." It was the philosophy of a leader with a precocious management pedigree. Breitling's new equity group owners (first CVC Capital Partners in 2017, then Partners Group in 2022) had chosen Georges as a man of the times. He made bold moves: taking control of Breitling's messaging with global summits; broadening its appeal with new models in feminine and unisex styles; and making solid commitments to Breitling's heritage, inclusivity, and sustainability. Georges set out a vision "to be more relaxed, informal, cooler, younger, and fresher." Breitling, he predicted, was on its way to becoming a top-five Swiss watch brand and the leader of a newly defined neo-luxury market.

ABOVE
*Alfred Gantner co-founder of Partners Group (left) and Breitling CEO Georges Kern*

# 109

## CHANGING HANDS: THEODORE SCHNEIDER TO CVC CAPITAL PARTNERS, PARTNERS GROUP, AND GEORGES KERN

For Theodore Schneider, handing control of the company he had made his own was a hard decision. Breitling's sales were on the rise, but the landscape of luxury retailing had changed, digital marketing had taken over from handshake deals, and the time was right for new leadership.

The statements issued in 2017 were designed to inspire confidence, but one phrase from Theodore stands out: the sale of 80 percent of his shares to CVC Capital Partners "will help unlock Breitling's full potential."

Like Willy Breitling before him when he sold to Ernest Schneider, Theodore also had an interest in seeing Breitling maintain its independence outside of the big luxury conglomerates. Private equity provided both the security and autonomy Breitling would need to thrive.

In a surprise move, Richemont's head of watchmaking, Georges Kern, was announced as CEO. With 25 years of impressive—and often disruptive—luxury watch industry leadership behind him, Georges's appointment signaled the start of a new era. Breitling would be redefined as the leader of modern "casual, inclusive, sustainable luxury."

It soon became clear what this meant in practice; the testosterone-fueled promotions of the previous decades gave way to informal Breitling Summits, *#Squadonamission* brought together inspiring ambassadors, and new boutiques showed off heritage-inspired watches in a distinctive industrial-loft setting.

By 2022, the ownership would change again, the Swiss-based Partners Group increasing its stake to become the majority shareholder. But what would remain unchanged was the new direction.

# 110

## CRAFTING A NEW IDENTITY

"We changed the whole corporate identity," is how Georges Kern summed up his first few years at Breitling. A decision was taken in the early days that the former laser focus on aviation was proving a limiting factor. From now on Breitling would be a generalist brand, appealing to a wide range of customers. "We're still leaders in pilot's watches," he said. "But history shows us that we were much more than that."

To signal that intention, there would be major improvements in every area of the company, from the watch models on sale to the design of boutiques, and the visual cues that identify the brand.

Use of the wings and anchor logo, designed for Ernest Schneider in the early 1980s, was scaled back and replaced on most models by the "script B" that had been used since the 1940s. Sustainability and inclusivity became watchwords, and Breitling's distinctive yellow tied the story together in ads, displays, and online.

"The whole company became less, I would say, one-dimensional," Georges said, six years into the journey.

*BELOW*
*Breitling's new logos were based on designs from the thirties and forties*

# III

## REDISCOVERING HERITAGE

It was only after Georges Kern took charge that he discovered models from Breitling's past that had, for most people, been all but forgotten.

"I saw these products from the 1930s to 1980s, and I thought, 'Oh my god, this would be a home run,'" he said of coming across *@watchfred* on Instagram.

It was a moment that the owner of that handle, and of those watches, had been dreaming of for years. Fred Mandelbaum, a tech entrepreneur in Austria and one of the world's foremost chronograph collectors, had a penchant for pieces from the Willy Breitling era. He had been operating in a separate universe to the future-focused Schneiders, but had longed to see heritage reinstated at the brand.

Within two weeks of starting, Georges struck up a correspondence with the collector, whose tentative sign off on one early email was "with cautious hope."

The two watch obsessives met in Vienna where Georges saw, spread out on Mandelbaum's boardroom table, not just Breitling's past, but also its future. Land and sea watches were represented alongside those meant for the air. And what most inspired the new CEO were Willy Breitling's elegant Premier watches.

It was a meeting of minds that would lead to extensive consultation on re-editions, the reintroduction of design cues not seen for half a century or more, and ultimately Fred's appointment as Breitling's official historian.

LEFT
*From left, collector Fred Mandelbaum, Breitling Chief of Staff Alexander Middelmann, and CEO Georges Kern at their fortuitous meeting in Vienna*

*ABOVE*
*The Superocean Heritage 57 was among the first collections to get the modern-retro treatment*

# 112

## MODERN RETRO

The meeting between Georges Kern and watch collector Fred Mandelbaum in the early days of Breitling's new ownership changed the track of development and led to a new aesthetic that became known as "modern retro."

The history of the elegant Premier dress watches that Willy Breitling had developed in the 1940s had been lost to all but a niche subset of collectors. Georges was so impressed, he pledged not only to relaunch the model, but to do so within a year.

The Premier revival was a hit. Instead of a reproduction, the watch that had taken the chrono "from purpose to style" in Willy Breitling's era was translated into a contemporary format.

In describing modern retro, Georges compared it to the latest Porsche 911, a classic with a historic pedigree, but up-to-date and instantly recognizable. He saw the new Breitling models in the same light: "We've modernized them in such a way that you have classic elements, but with a modern touch."

# 113 BREITLING HISTORY ON TOUR

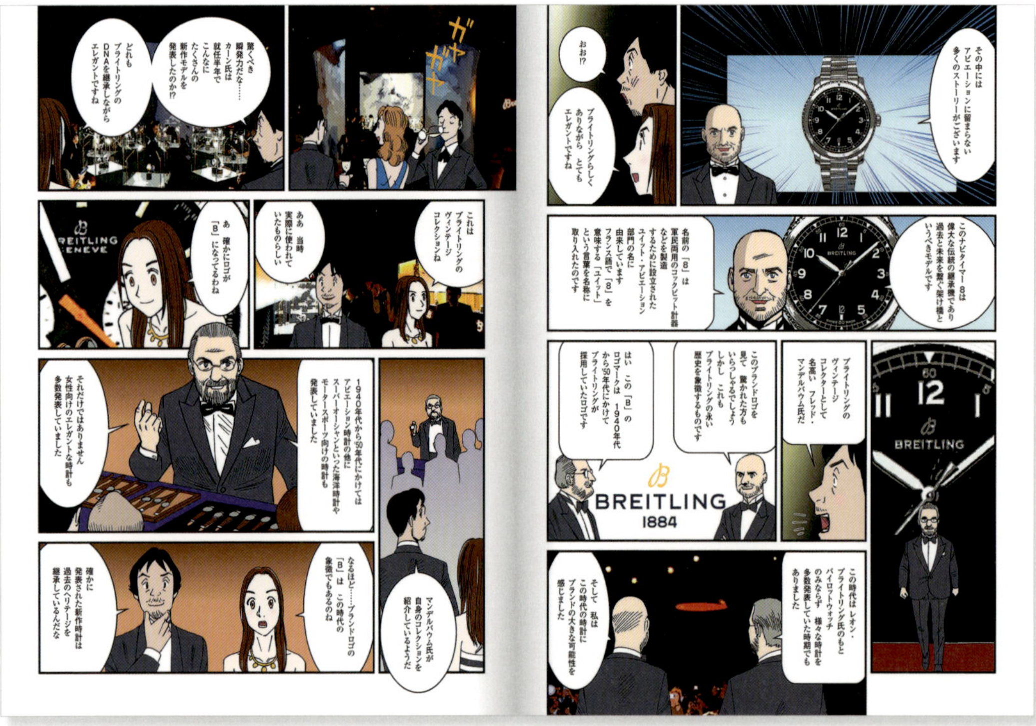


*LEFT*
*Comic featuring Georges Kern and Fred Mandelbaum published in the* Tokei Begin*, Japanese watch magazine, 2018*

"It began with Georges Kern reaching out to me in a 2017 phone call to say he was taking over Breitling and could I help him in rediscovering the brand heritage. For years Breitling had been reined in to a small segment: large pilot watches. But the roots of the brand were much wider: they were air, land, and sea. Sports watches, dive watches, and, of course, pilot watches. That year, we set out on roadshows in Shanghai, New York, and Zurich to present the new Breitling and its unbelievably deep back catalog of innovation. This comic, for example, was done by a Japanese media outlet that attended the event in Shanghai. In Zurich, I had the pleasure of meeting Willy Breitling's son, Gregory. Most of the brand's foundational pieces were thanks to Willy, and one of the nicest things that happened was to see Gregory so moved as we recognized his father's spirit of innovation and the importance he held in the brand's evolution. Almost everyone I spoke with on those tours had the same reaction: that they were discovering an unknown treasure. It was a collector's dream come true."

**FRED MANDELBAUM**

*A longtime Breitling collector and current brand historian, Mandelbaum instructs widely on heritage and acts as historical advisor to Breitling's design department.*

# 114

## INDUSTRIAL LOFT REVOLUTION

When you walk into a Breitling boutique and instantly sense that you belong there, the designers know they've done their job. "It feels like I am at a friend's contemporary urban loft downtown," is how Breitling's U.S. president, Thierry Prissert, described the flagship Madison Avenue boutique in Manhattan.

Vintage decor and artwork, streamlined modern design, and bright pops of Breitling yellow highlight the brand's history in dedicated zones for air, land, and sea. It's part aircraft hangar, part beach cabana, with more than a hint of leatherwork and dashboards from the glory days of motor racing. And if there's no pressure to buy, that's deliberate too. High stools and low couches encourage relaxed conversations, while motorbikes, surfboards, and even pool tables provide a comfortable and inclusive space to indulge in a little neo-luxury.

Breitling's modern-retro look has been rolled out across the globe with one overriding instruction to staff: "There is no pressure here, only an opportunity for people to discover the brand at their own pace, while having a great time."

*BELOW*
***Breitling's Manchester boutique***

# 115

*“People may not know why a space makes them feel a certain way. It’s a combination of materials, colors, lighting, fragrance, music, service, and, of course, good design. We touch all senses and, in the end, want people to think, ‘I want to live here. I want to be like this.’”*

*ALEXANDRA WEIS, BREITLING GLOBAL DIRECTOR OF TRADE MARKETING*

# 116

## THE RETURN OF AIR, LAND, AND SEA

In the 1950s, Willy Breitling ran ads for "Breitling Time: In the air, on the ground, under the sea," and asked, "Why not on your wrist?" It was a question that Georges Kern asked again as he took stock of Breitling's catalog six decades later.

Theodore Schneider had likened Breitling to a shark in the Swiss watch industry—he even had yellow-finned models produced to hand out at the Baselworld watch fair—but Georges could see that the brand's relentless focus on aviation was now confining that shark to a swimming pool.

At the same time as slimming down the number of models in production, Georges put them back into the three historic brand universes of air, land, and sea. For watches that spanned more than one domain, he added two extra segments: Professional and All-Purpose.

The rearrangement of the catalog was a key part of the brand's new direction. "Look at some other brands," Georges said, "You buy one product, you basically bought the brand, and this is absolutely not the case at Breitling."

*BELOW*
*Georges Kern announcing the return of the three historic Breitling universes*

ABOVE
*The all-star squad, from left: pro basketball player Giannis Antetokounmpo, two-time winter games gold medalist Chloe Kim, and pro footballer Erling Haaland*

# 117

## MEET THE SQUADS

How to promote the generalist Breitling was a question that required considerable thought. The new commitment was to casual, inclusive, sustainable luxury. Conveying that measured tone in the noise and bluster of modern media was a challenge.

The solution was to replace individual celebrity endorsements with "squads" of masters in their respective fields, from sports to the arts. The concept of *#Squadonamission* was born.

The Cinema Squad was the first, with the star power of actors Charlize Theron, Brad Pitt, and Adam Driver; all articulate, intelligent, and easygoing. Then came the Spotlight, Explorer, Aviation Pioneer, Triathlon, Navitimer, and all-star squads.

The Surfer Squad, formed in 2018, captured the essence of the idea: Kelly Slater, Stephanie Gilmore, and Sally Fitzgibbons were not only among the best in their sport, but they actively shared Breitling's commitment to maintaining clean oceans and beaches.

Astronaut Scott Kelly, from the Aviation Pioneer Squad, believes the ethos of working together is key to his success. "It is absolutely critical that you're part of a team," he said. "Part of a squad."

## #Squadonamission

*Idiom*

Three recognized individuals in a shared field, united in a single purpose. This team approach has been employed in Breitling's advertising since 2018 as an alternative to traditional celebrity endorsements.

# 119 OLLIE CRAWFORD: A HUMBLE WARRIOR

LEFT
*Three generations of P-40 Warhawk pilots. From left, Ollie Crawford, Taylor Stevenson, and Ray Kinney*

“My dad met Ray Kinney in the early seventies. Ray had always been a pilot and my dad had always wanted to fly. They bought a T-6 Texan together after Dad spotted it at an airshow. Two weeks later, he was taking flying lessons.

Ray is my aviation mentor. I got my pilot's certificate on my sixteenth birthday because of him. Dad and Ray had a mentor too, Ollie Crawford, who joined the U.S. Army Air Force during World War II. He flew the Curtiss P-40 Warhawk for the first time at 19 and the last time at 80. He was a constant in serving veterans, was honored with accolades, and is the reason we have an Air Force Memorial in Washington, D.C., today.

For years, Dad, Ray, and Ollie were the P-40's three musketeers at airshows. They learned everything from Ollie. Then in 2019, Breitling put out a call for a World War II pilot for their Aviator 8 Curtiss P-40 Warhawk watch campaign. When I told our story, it evolved from one veteran to the whole three-generation crew. Ten days later, we were in San Antonio filming. Ollie was ecstatic.

The shoot was great. Then, Breitling called with an invitation to the watch's launch event—in Beijing! Next thing, we're in China, Ollie sharing stories of his 70-plus years in aviation. The room is filled with countless influential people, but it's clear Ollie is the rock star. Even Brad Pitt gets in line to speak to him.

Ollie passed away just a few months later, on July 21, 2019. More than a successful entrepreneur, his life's work had been for veterans. These humble warriors are fading, but Ollie's last chapter was the greatest send-off for a truly amazing man.”

**TAYLOR STEVENSON**

*A lawyer who moonlights as an airshow pilot, Stevenson has been flying vintage aircraft since he was 16. His plane of choice is the legendary Curtiss P-40 Warhawk.*

20
17

20
24

# 120

## BRAND BUILDING IN THE TIME OF COVID

If there was a moment that crystallized Breitling's new position as a leader, not a follower, it came in a statement from Georges Kern in April 2019: "We will not be exhibiting at Baselworld in 2020."

It was a major disruption to the accepted way of doing business in the watch world. From now on, Breitling's developments would be revealed to journalists, customers, and an increasingly attentive industry, not as one among many at the annual Swiss watch fair but in regular in-person summits.

Then came the COVID-19 pandemic, leaving businesses shuttered, silent, and stumped. With the world on lockdown, Breitling took its new idea of the summit online.

The first Summit Webcast in April 2020 saw Georges Kern pledging his support for global efforts to contain the virus, and then came a stream of unveilings: the Superocean Heritage 57 Rainbow Edition capturing the international symbol of hope in the crisis; the Navitimer 35 showing the importance of women's collections; and a complete redesign of the Chronomat. Simultaneously, information landed in the inboxes of journalists and influencers, lighting up social media. "In every objective and subjective way, this was a success," one watch journalist proclaimed. "Breitling has every reason to be delighted and congratulated."

*BELOW*
*Georges Kern in virtual conversation with Breitling ambassador, principal dancer Misty Copeland*

*ABOVE*
*The Founders Squad, made up of deep-fake reproductions of Leon, Gaston, and Willy Breitling*

# 121

## BREITLING RESURRECTION: FOUNDERS IN THE DIGITAL AGE

Breitling's fourth Summit Webcast to introduce the redesigned Premier collection took a leap into the digital deep end when it introduced the Founders Squad—Leon, Gaston, and Willy Breitling—who had been digitally resurrected.

Georges Kern orchestrated a "deep fake" sit-down with the trio that was part history lesson, part tech showcase. It was a move that split the room: some applauded the innovative homage, while others found the seance a tad eerie.

But love it or loathe it, one thing is for sure: it got people's attention. Breitling's founding fathers were back for an encore, whether you were ready for them or not.

2017

# 122

2024

# 2020
# CHRONOMAT B01 42
## SET TO SOAR ONCE AGAIN

When the Chronomat was designed in the early 1980s, its crown, rider tabs, and the beauty of its lines were touches of genius. The new Chronomat brought that genius up-to-date. The rider tabs could still provide a countdown or a count up, but the bezel was perfectly streamlined. At 42 mm, with Breitling's Manufacture Caliber 01, a 200-meter water resistance, and an all-new Rouleaux bracelet, the Chronomat re-staked its claim as the ultimate all-purpose watch.

# 123

## BRAD PITT: STAR RESET

In a 2019 *GQ* cover story, Brad Pitt, Hollywood's quintessential leading man, sported a 1969 Breitling Top Time, a watch as enduring as his decades-spanning career. From the untamed backdrop of *Legends of the Fall* to the starlit hustle of *Once Upon a Time in Hollywood*, Pitt's journey has been a versatile odyssey of roles. In his years as a Breitling ambassador, he donned his share of new watches in the brand's campaigns (such as this one for the Chronomat, shot by Peter Lindbergh), but Pitt liked to dip into the archives when off duty. His pick of the vintage Top Time was telling: rugged, refined, and effortlessly cool, just like the man himself.

124

## WE DID THAT

# BREITLIGHT

In the world of Swiss watchmaking, a new star was born—Breitlight. It all began with BIWI, a company on a mission to beef up the ends of their rubber straps. Their scientists, tasked with creating a titanium-like material without the titanium price tag, ended up outdoing themselves. The result? An ultra-light carbon-fiber composite stronger than titanium, heat-resistant to 150 degrees Celsius, and easily injection-molded and machined. Theodore Schneider got his hands on this wonder material—then called Titaplast—at Baselworld 2014 where BIWI was billing it as "the strongest polymer in the world." Theodore, recalling how Willy Breitling once revolutionized the 1970s Sprint with a featherweight resin case, didn't hesitate. He snagged the exclusive watchmaking rights—snappily rebranding it "Breitlight." Months later, the ultralight Avenger Hurricane was on the drawing board. Skip ahead to 2020: Georges Kern makes Breitlight the go-to for the Endurance Pro, echoing the Sprint's legacy, tailored for today's sports aficionados.

*LEFT*
*World champion triathlete Daniela Ryf*

20
17

# 125

20
24

# 2020
# ENDURANCE PRO
## THE PACE SETTER

Breitling's Endurance Pro burst onto the scene in 2020, fitting right in with the pandemic-sparked athleisure trend. The watch wasn't just about keeping time but urging you out when socializing was on shutdown and athletics was, for many, the only outlet. A fun, high-viz watch with a 44-millimeter ultralight Breitlight case, oversized lumed numerals, and an array of colorful rubber straps, it was—and remains—the epitome of athletic style, suited to sprinters and strollers alike.

# 126

## THINKING INSIDE THE BOX

When Breitling's sustainable watch box hit boutiques in 2020, everyone sat up and took notice. Its composition in 100 percent recycled PET diverted plastic bottles from landfills, its ingenious flat-fold construction made it efficient to transport, and its interior display material, used to prop up the watch for the ideal presentation, played double duty as a convenient travel pouch.

Breitling would have many other breakthrough moments on the sustainability front, including becoming the first in the watch industry to align its greenhouse-gas-reduction targets to the leading Science Based Targets initiative's Corporate Net-Zero Standard. And while most applauded the brand's commitment, the box continued to garner debate.

Gen Z customers loved it, even if the big, heavy boxes of old were lamented by some. Those who insisted could still have one—with a strong suggestion to contribute to Breitling's carbon-offset partner.

It was a stake in the ground, and as Breitling's global director of sustainability, Aurelia Figueroa, put it, "No one brand can solve the climate crisis, but we can each do the most we can in our sphere of influence. Sustainability is the greatest challenge—and opportunity—of our time."

*BELOW*
*Breitling's flat-fold watch box, made from recycled PET*

*ABOVE*
***Surfing, as represented by the Surfer Squad (from left, Sally Fitzgibbons, Kelly Slater, and Stephanie Gilmore), was chosen for its inclusivity***

# 127

## NEO LUXURY

Breitling's 2017 shift to "neo-luxury," as Georges Kern describes it, mixes casualness, inclusivity, and sustainability. "We are exclusive by price, but we don't want to be exclusive by arrogance," he asserts. This mindset aligns with the social values and financial clout of Millennials and Gen Z, shaping Breitling's diverse watch catalog and brand ethos. Ambassadors from relatable fields, eco-conscious packaging, and blockchain traceability complement boutiques reminiscent of stylish apartments, where sneaker-clad staff enhance the brand's polished yet approachable vibe.

2017
2024

# 128

## 2022

# NAVITIMER B01 CHRONOGRAPH 43

### 70TH ANNIVERSARY REDESIGN

The reimagined Navitimer made its grand entrance on its seventieth birthday, unveiled in the air aboard three Swiss International Air Lines flights to Geneva in a special "in-flight entertainment" edition of the Summit Webcast. The timepiece wove together the new and the nostalgic, pairing a sleek, modern silhouette and contemporary dial colors with the return of the classic AOPA insignia. Always a risk to upend an icon, the move hit the mark by preserving the Navi's spot-across-a-room design while giving it new life.

# 129

## MISTY COPELAND: BORN TO DANCE

Misty Copeland's journey, from a childhood marked by adversity to the pinnacle of ballet as the first African American principal dancer in the American Ballet Theatre, is a tale of grace and grit. Beginning ballet at the late age of 13, Misty demonstrated a raw, prodigious talent that took her from her first dance lesson to performing professionally in the span of a year. As part of Breitling's Navitimer Squad, she appeared in the Navitimer's seventieth-anniversary "For the Journey" campaign with the poise of a seasoned pro. Then, in a moment as raw and real as her ascent, Copeland recounted her journey story, embodying the roles of a principal dancer, author, mentor, and—in a captivating turn—as a mother-to-be.

20
17

20
24

# 130

## MODERN MARKETING

There's an old adage that it's not the size of your marketing budget that counts, but where you spend it. For decades Breitling's money had gone toward spectacular aviation events, from world record balloon flights to sponsoring a jet display team.

Becoming cool, inclusive, and generalist meant new methods of marketing. Where there had been no e-commerce—until 2017, you could not buy from Breitling online—a digital presence was built from the ground up. Inherited sponsorship deals ended, and 40 percent of the marketing budget was earmarked for digital channels, while new forms of out-of-home advertising transformed iconic spaces, from the Burj Khalifa in Dubai to Times Square in New York.

Like Willy Breitling, who used the Breitling yellow to stand out in the world of black-and-white print, or Theodore Schneider, who emblazoned the brand name on the Orbiter balloon, staying relevant is a constant process, and Georges Kern likes to use a maxim that will never grow old: "What was forward thinking five or 10 years ago is not forward thinking now."

# 131 60 YEARS OF THE COSMONAUTE

“Everyone at NASA had been hunting for the best possible watch for space travel. My dad, the Mercury 7 astronaut Scott Carpenter, hadn't much liked any of those proffered by manufacturers' representatives. But then he saw the Navitimer, the 'ultimate wrist-worn computer for pilots.'

After he was assigned his mission, my father wrote to Willy Breitling: 'I love your watch. Could you make one with a 24-hour display?' He asked for other modifications suitable for space travel. *Yes*, was the reply. Willy Breitling made the watch to my dad's specifications, and the reconfigured Navitimer, from then on dubbed the Cosmonaute, flew into space on his left wrist.

Scott Carpenter and his Cosmonaute survived spaceflight from launch to splashdown to a difficult capsule egress through the narrow nose. Settling safely in the raft, my dad flopped on his back, a tethered *Aurora 7* capsule bobbing on the Atlantic before him. He glanced at the timepiece on his wrist. Before folding his arms behind his head, he said to himself, 'Man,' and pondered his five unforgettable hours.

U.S. Navy choppers arrived from a distant USS *Intrepid* and winched him to safety and, eventually, home.

That's how my dad became a watch designer, the designer of the first Swiss wristwatch to be flown in space. Did I say it was beautiful? It is.”

**KRIS STOEVER**

Coauthor of *For Spacious Skies: The Uncommon Journey of a Mercury Astronaut* with her astronaut father, Stoever discussed his historic space flight during Breitling's 2022 event marking its sixtieth anniversary.

2017

2024

# 132

# 2022 NAVITIMER COSMONAUTE

## 60TH ANNIVERSARY REDESIGN

When Mercury 7 astronaut Scott Carpenter asked Willy Breitling to make a modified Navitimer for his upcoming space mission, Willy jumped at the challenge. Carpenter loved the slide rule but had no need for the tachymeter. Rather than a 12-hour scale, he asked for 24 hours to tell day from night in space. The unique Navitimer accompanied Carpenter on an orbital journey on May 24, 1962, becoming the world's first space-going wrist chronograph. This sixtieth-anniversary watch paid tribute to the historic flight in a limited-edition 2022 release.

20
17

20
24

133

WE DID THAT

# SUPER CHRONOMAT ORIGINS

Origins is the name given to Breitling's commitment to roll out artisanal gold and lab-grown diamonds across its watch portfolio. Billed as a logical progression toward sustainability and transparency, Origins was launched with a striking 38-millimeter Super Chronomat. Owners can trace their watch's gold and diamonds in each watch's NFT, with the supply-chain steps independently verified. The debut edition featured gold sourced from a single Colombian mine that met the Swiss Better Gold Association's commitments to improving conditions in its local communities. The lab-grown diamonds, created by applying gas and heat to a diamond slice in a vacuum, are identical to mined diamonds, but free of association with conflict or human rights abuses. What Breitling dubbed as its "better gold" and "better diamonds" are seen as a further expression of its concept of neo-luxury, setting a more visible course through the too-often-opaque world of precious material provenance.

20
17

# 134

20
24

## 2023

# NAVITIMER AUTOMATIC 36

### SUSTAINABLY CHIC

Breitling introduced the Navitimer Automatic 36 and 32 as a collection of three-hand Navitimers for women that combined its iconic design with elevated precious materials. This mother-of-pearl dial variant follows the Origins model, with gold sourced from small-scale mines that meet the Swiss Better Gold Association's exacting criteria, and traceable, lab-grown diamonds—a stylish and sustainable representation of the Breitling icon.

# 135

## CHARLIZE THERON: THE ART OF TRANSFORMATION

Charlize Theron's journey from the open vistas of Benoni, South Africa, to the spotlights of Hollywood reads like a script she might have once brought to life—full of tenacity and relentless ambition. With performances that range from the harrowing drama *Monster* to dystopian action film *Mad Max: Fury Road*, Theron joined Breitling in 2018, bringing the same authenticity to her role as ambassador as she does to her characters on screen, continuing to inspire the next generation of talent.

20
17

20
24

# 136

## “Analog watches are the ultimate anti-metaverse, and that’s precisely why they are in demand.”

*GEORGES KERN*

20
17

# 137

20
24

2024

# AEROSPACE B70 ORBITER

## JUBILEE JOURNEY

The Aerospace B70 Orbiter honors the 25th anniversary of the Breitling Orbiter 3's historic nonstop balloon flight around the world, piloted by Bertrand Piccard and Brian Jones. This titanium tribute—Breitling's first watch powered by the manufacture B70 SuperQuartz movement—features an orange dial the same color as the original Orbiter 3 capsule. What makes it a living tribute: each watch carries a fragment of the original balloon, visible through the open caseback.

ORBITER 3

# 138

## BERTRAND PICCARD: CLEAN TECH VOYAGER

Born into a family of explorers, Bertrand Piccard has carved his own path by championing sustainable development and clean technologies. With feats like circumnavigating the globe in the Breitling Orbiter 3 balloon in 1999 and by solar-powered aircraft in 2016, he seeks to raise awareness and prompt action on environmental issues. Piccard's Solar Impulse Foundation looks at climate solutions through the lens of profitability, highlighted by the Solar Impulse Efficient Solutions label, certifying products that are both economically viable and environmentally sound. As he puts it, "We shouldn't look at the climate crisis as a problem requiring sacrifice, but as an opportunity to do better than we ever have before. It's our chance to make our world more efficient."

# 139

## THE B19: A CENTURY IN MOTION

After the success of the Manufacture Caliber 01 and its suite of exclusive follow-up movements, Breitling set out to launch an even more complicated edition for its 140th anniversary—the B19. What makes this caliber exceptional—much like the 140-year-old brand itself—is its stamina. This piece of craftsmanship, which took two years of development to create, features a perpetual calendar, one of the most difficult-to-execute complications—and a first in Breitling history. Once it's running, the calendar doesn't need a major manual adjustment for 100 years, not even during leap years. However, the intention behind the B19 wasn't solely to showcase technical innovation but to honor the visionary spirit of Leon Breitling, who opened the Montbrillant Watch Manufactory in La Chaux-de-Fonds in 1893—the building's image is now engraved on the movement's rotor. Ivan Greguitch, director of product development at Breitling, notes, "The B19 is a celebration of savoir-faire spanning 140 years, breathing new life into Leon Breitling's legacy. It hints at where Breitling is headed while simultaneously honoring its past."

*BELOW*
*The B19 perpetual calendar movement*

# 140

## THIS IS JUST THE BEGINNING

Breitling CEO Georges Kern has been asked a lot about his standard sign off: "And remember... this is just the beginning." It's been parodied by Charlize Theron and Brad Pitt in his webcasts; a host of media have tried to beat him to the punch at press events. So where does the catchphrase come from? "We have this huge history," Kern said. "Huge back catalog. Huge plans. It's endless what lies in our past and what we have in store for the future of Breitling. That's why every moment is just the beginning."

## ACKNOWLEDGMENTS

Breitling wishes to thank the Breitling family, who generously opened their archives for the creation of this book, granting us access to their vast collection of personal photographs, documents, and anecdotes. We also owe our sincerest gratitude to the many people within the Breitling organization, past and present, who made this publication possible: Alfred Gantner, Alexander Dibelius, Daniel Piadur, Georges Kern, Nasr Benaissa, Alexander Middelmann, Laura Amarelle, Thierry Prissert, Gianfranco Gentile, Jennifer Bochud, Paul Mulocher, Lars Summers, Theresa Poll, Lara Kazakos, Aileen Askari Doan, Jeremy Weingart, Kalli Cheslock, Natacha Matter, Alexandra Weis, Hugo Hemeray, Lindsay Paterson, Toshitaka Ariyoshi, Manami Taniguchi, Kim Jin, Andy Su, Mathilde Bernard, Reto Krattiger, Anne-Marie Rerat, Emigliano Grisoni, Marion Schnyder, Michael Hefti, Simon Kehl, Eva Krisper, Tilen Zonta, Ben Balmer, and Theodore Schneider.

# CREDITS

pp. 12, 20 [bottom], 21, 34, 40, 46, 62–63, 67 [right], 76, 82, 87, 88, 89, 108, 116–117, 122, 141: Courtesy the Breitling Family [All rights reserved]

p. 13: © Mémoires d'Ici, Fonds Oliver Wileczelek – Éditeur Neuchâtel: Phototypie, no. 7935

p. 14: © Mémoires d'Ici, Famille Emile Herrli

pp. 15 [right], 18–19, 20 [top], 25, 27, 55, 56, 60–61, 65, 66, 67 [left], 77, 78, 79, 90–91, 125, 128–129, 131, 132 [bottom], 133, 139, 140 [bottom], 144, 154, 155, 186, 191 [bottom], 203, 204, 212 [© James Dietz], 213, 225, 228 [© Tokei Begin magazine], 229, 237, 246, 252, 253, 256, 268: © Breitling Archive [All rights reserved]

p. 15 [left]: © Musée de Saint-Imier

pp. 16–17: © Musée d'histoire, Ville de La Chaux-de-Fonds, Switzerland

pp. 22–23: © Louis Van Oeyen/Western Reserve Historical Society/Getty Images

pp. 26, 39, 47: Swiss Federal Institute of Intellectual Property

p. 35: © Archivio storico Fondazione Corriere della Sera

p. 38: © Agence Meurisse/Bibliothèque nationale de France

pp. 50, 110–111: © Keystone View Company/Archive Photos/Getty Images

p. 57: © De Luan/Alamy Stock Foto/Ipa Agency

p. 93: © "Thirteen Steps, Orthodox Judaism in America Comes of Age: My Life and Times" by Rabbi Joseph Karasick [OU Press]

pp. 100–101: © Michael Ochs Archives/Getty Images

pp. 106–107: © Mondadori Portfolio/© 20thCentFox/ Courtesy Everett Collection

p. 123: © Mondadori Portfolio/Keystone AG/Jules Vogt

p. 132 [top]: © Federation of the Swiss Watch Industry

p. 140 [top]: © Fred Mandelbaum

p. 149: © unknown/Signatur: Sozarch_F_5032-Fd-0147, Courtesy Schweizerisches Sozialarchiv

pp. 158–159: © Hulton Archive/Getty Images

p. 161: © Dino Fracchia/Alamy Stock Photo/Ipa Agency

pp. 168–169: © Ann Summa/Getty Images

pp. 171, 172 [top]: © Alexander Babic

pp. 172 [bottom], 205, 208–209, 219: © Katsuhiko Tokunaga

p. 173: © Alessandro Barteletti

p. 177: © Kazuyuki Takahashi

pp. 180–181: © Nigel Parry

p. 187: © Contrôle Officiel Suisse des Chronomètres

p. 189: © Nicolas Le Corre, Courtesy Solar Impulse

p. 190: © Piccard B. Jones, Courtesy Solar Impulse

p. 191 [top]: © Martin Rütschi, Courtesy Solar Impulse

p. 192: © Thomas Buchwalder

p. 193: © Venzin+Bühler Fotografen

p. 195: © Valeriano Di Domenico

pp. 200–201, 211: © Courtesy Airborne Films

p. 206: © Janine Menlove

pp. 126, 127, 207 [© Scott Kelly]: Courtesy NASA Archives

pp. 216–217: © Fiona Hanson/PA/Alamy Stock Foto/ Ipa Agency

p. 224: © Dan Cermak

p. 226: © René Kesting

p. 230: © Milton Tan

p. 232: © Adrian Bretscher/GettyImages

pp. 233, 250–251, 260–261: © Matthew Brookes

p. 235: © Mike Shore

p. 236: © Spring Studios

pp. 240–241: © Eric Guillemain

pp. 242, 247: © Dougal Paterson

p. 253 [portrait]: © Harold Cunningham

p. 263: © Charley Gallay/GettyImages

pp. 266–267: © Anders Overgaard

p. 269: © Remy Steiner

Concept and story curation: Fred Mandelbaum, Natasha Mekhail

Editing: Natasha Mekhail

Art direction and graphic design: Jason Treanor

Publishing management: Anne-Lise Ensminger

Watch photography: Elias Hartmann

Archival research: Tanja Jedlitschka

Imagery database: Christoph Kainzner

Image clearance and iconographic research: Simona Girella

Prepress and lithography: Images 3

Contributors: Carol Besler, Gregory Breitling, Talia Farghaly, Kevin T. Kelly, Atsushi Kimbara, Christopher Korchin, Fred Mandelbaum, Jeff Stein, Taylor Stevenson, Kris Stoever, Gerard Tubb, Aaron Voyles



Distributed in English throughout the World
by Rizzoli International Publications Inc.
49 West 27th Street
New York, NY 10001
www.rizzoliusa.com

ISBN: 9788891841773

2025 2026 2027 / 10 9 8 7 6 5 4 3 2

First edition: October 2024



This volume was printed at Errestampa S.r.l.
Via Portico 27, Orio al Serio, Bergamo
Printed in Italy

The authorized representative in the EU for product safety and compliance is Mondadori Libri S.p.A., via Gian Battista Vico 42, Milan, Italy, 20123.
www.mondadori.it

Visit us online:
Instagram.com/RizzoliBooks
Facebook.com/RizzoliNewYork
X: @Rizzoli_Books
Youtube.com/user/RizzoliNY